A WALK AMONG GIANTS

TREKKING AROUND THE ANNAPURNA CIRCUIT

DAVID OXLEY

Published by David Oxley

© 2024

All rights reserved. No part of this book may be reproduced or modified in any form, including photocopying, recording, or by any information storage and retrieval system, without permission in writing from the publisher.

Although the author is an experienced altitude trekker, he is not a medical doctor or health professional so any advice given should also be discussed with your doctor.

The author is not a qualified mountain guide, so any advice given on route guidance should be discussed with a qualified professional mountain guide.

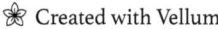 Created with Vellum

*Dedicated to Deb, my long-suffering wife,
who kept me sane when situations
went pear-shaped and shared the joy
of our adventure trekking in the Himalayas.*

INTRODUCTION

This is an account of an adventure my wife Deb and I had in 2016 in Nepal, where we trekked the Annapurna Circuit in its entirety. Our journey was undertaken completely independently and without guides or porters.

I had lost my Dad the year before which came as a massive shock to my system; a real wake-up call. My Grandparents had died 25 years previously, and now my Dad. I suppose I thought, I'm next in line. This realisation of my impending mortality prompted me to take early retirement from my teaching post and to do something exciting with my life before eternity came crashing in. I was almost 60 when we did this trip, and I wanted to drag myself around the Himalayas before I got too old and finally kicked the bucket.

I learned a lot about myself, and Deb, during our trek up and down the mountain trails of Nepal, meeting some of its lovely people, and visiting its busy cities. I had many moments that bordered on complete madness and quickly came to understand that I am not one of life's natural travellers and that my greatest asset is my long-suffering wife

Deb, without whom I would probably not have completed the trek.

I also found many connections on the trek to my younger life and I try to intertwine these anecdotes throughout the book in an attempt to bind my present to my past. I hope you will find humour within these pages and perhaps even a little wisdom, but I hope most of all you will find inspiration to undertake an adventure of your own, perhaps even a trip to Nepal. I like to think that, as a human being, husband and father, I am a work in progress; the time we both spent in Nepal has certainly changed me as a person and given me a better perspective on the world and life.

This book is not intended as a substitute for a good guidebook; however, I do hope it will offer the reader an insight into the gentle art of trekking, and throw a spotlight onto the glorious country that is Nepal, and the wonderful Nepalese people.

CONTENTS

PART I
THE START OF IT ALL

1. My Kids Are Trying To Kill Me ... 3
2. On Our Way At Last ... 14
3. Getting To The Start Line ... 24

PART II
THE TREK BEGINS

4. Rotten Russians And A Giant Spider ... 33
5. The Three Amigos And Police Patrols ... 45
6. Trouble With Dogs ... 56
7. At The Edges Of Life ... 66
8. Onwards And Upwards ... 80
9. A Rag Doll And A Pile Of Poo ... 91

PART III
ENTERING MUSTANG

10. The High Pass ... 103
11. The Three Witches Of Chhairo ... 115
12. The Guns Of Kalopani ... 130
13. Going Up In The World ... 144
14. Poon Hill, Bears And Pool ... 155
15. Steps, Americans And Dizzy Spells ... 165
16. Our Last Day Trekking ... 177

PART IV
A TALE OF TWO CITIES

17. A Bus, A Mouse And A Prostate ... 189
18. The Coffee Man And Trouble With Monkeys ... 203
19. I See Dead People ... 219
20. Homeward Bound ... 230

Epilogue ... 234

Acknowledgments	237
Untitled	239

PART I

THE START OF IT ALL

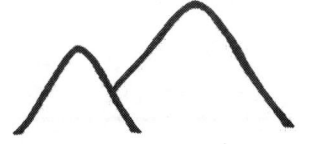

1

MY KIDS ARE TRYING TO KILL ME

Comfort zones. Nobody spoke about comfort zones when I was younger. In the seventies, a comfort zone would probably conjure up visions of a room full of large sofas with extra large cushions, hippy style; somewhere to lounge around, a bit like a toddler's soft play area. Now we all know it to be an emotional state of mind; a feeling of being at home; a place where our worries take a back seat; a stress-free frame of mind. It's a modern-day concept that's for sure. But, I like my comfort zone. I feel very comfortable in my comfort zone. That's not to say I'm totally against wandering out of it from time to time. I just don't want to wander too far out of it, so it becomes too difficult to get back. I like to be able to jump back into it, if things get too uncomfortable. On a sunny afternoon in early June 2016, I was prised out of my very comfortable comfort zone by my own loving family.

My wife Deb and I both retired earlier that year. I had done a twenty-year stint in secondary school as a physics teacher and Deb had taught the naughty kids in primary school. I was adapting well to retired life. I enjoyed the freedom of having time to do whatever I fancied doing. I even took up the gentle art of fly fishing. Deb on the other hand was struggling. She found the days dragging and missed the structure of her working life. She needed a project to get her teeth into. She was about to get just that.

It was a few days before Deb's birthday, and Father's Day was coming up too. So it was unusual, but not surprising when all four of our kids came round to see us at the same time. I say unusual because our eldest and youngest kids live and work two hundred miles away in Edinburgh. All seemed well at first. We did the usual catching up that families do when they haven't seen each other for a month or two. We talked about how their jobs were going, and if they had any holidays booked. All the usual things you would discuss to get up to date with each other's lives. Then I noticed a tension. There was something in the way the kids were glancing at each other. They were acting in a shifty kind of way. Nothing I could put my finger on, but something was not quite right. George, our eldest child, also known as General George, stood up and handed Deb a large white envelope. On the front was written 'To Mum and Dad, Happy Retirement.' This was unexpected. I didn't think kids gave their parents retirement gifts. Deb, not wanting to open the envelope herself, passed it to me. When we spoke about it afterwards we both thought the envelope would contain theatre tickets or maybe a booking for a weekend in a country hotel. Maybe it was a city break in Rome or Paris. Any of these would have been fantastic. I opened the envelope and simultaneously the door to my comfort zone creaked wide open. There in my sweaty, shaking hands were tickets to Kathmandu, Nepal. Return flights from Manchester to Kathmandu, October 17 to November 28, 2016. They had all been contributing each month. Not only had they bought the tickets, but they also gave us £2000 for expenses. Kathmandu! That's about 5000 miles outside my comfort zone. Oh my God, my kids are trying to kill me!

The weeks and months that followed were all about preparing for the trip. Deb was soon getting stuck into the research and making endless lists. In contrast, I was still in denial. Our first major decision to make was which trek in Nepal would we do. Deb had narrowed it down to just two choices: the Everest Base Camp trek and the Annapurna Circuit trek. These are by far the two most popular treks in Nepal. I was quite happy for her to decide which one, but I wasn't going to be allowed to take a back seat on this. She set me the task of reading up about these two treks. Now my lovely wife has given me many, many tasks over the forty years we've been together, and I've managed to dodge a fair few of them. However, I had a feeling this wasn't going to be one of them. So I diligently sat down with a couple of books: *Trekking in the Nepal Himalaya, a Lonely Planet book,* and *Trekking the Annapurna Circuit, a Himalayan Travel Guide.* This last book proved to be invaluable, as it had lots of detail on the new trails and how to avoid the newly constructed road. Reading these types of books is not something I find easy. There's just too much detail, and I just want an overview of what each of the treks is like. I just need to sit down with someone, who can talk me slowly through each of the treks. Does that make me lazy? Yes, it probably does. Several days after being given the job, Deb wanted my thoughts on which trek I fancied doing. I tried to sound like I'd done the research but she saw right through me. So she sat me down and slowly gave me an overview of the two treks.

She said, "To get to the start of the Everest Base Camp trek, we would need to catch a small plane from Kathmandu to Lukla, the most dangerous airport in the world. From there the Everest Base Camp Trek is walking up to Base Camp and then returning the same way." She did say more about it, but she'd lost me at 'the most dangerous airport in the world'. She continued to describe the Annapurna Circuit, "This trek is a horseshoe shape. It starts at Besisahar, which is at a low altitude, and works its way up to cross a high-altitude pass called Thorong La. Then the trail descends to lower altitudes again and finishes at a place called Nayapul." There was no doubt in my mind which trek I wanted to do. Even before she'd finished speaking I said, "Let's do the Annapurna Circuit." I think she would have rather done the Everest Trek, but on seeing my reaction to her descriptions of the treks, and in particular the 'most dangerous airport' comment, she agreed the Annapurna Circuit trek would be best.

The preparations weren't all about research, and what we would need, it was also about getting physically fit for the trek. We were in full agreement that we would do the trek by carrying all our gear; we didn't want to use porters. We would also walk independently; we didn't want to be part of a group, and we didn't want a guide. That doesn't mean that we are anti-social, well I suppose I am a little bit anti-social, it's just that we like to be in the hills and mountains on our own. People are great, but when we walk together, we can have long comfortable silences where we can experience the great outdoors without the constant chatter of being in a group. There's nothing wrong with walking in a group, it's just not for us. As they say, it's 'horses for courses' and these two horses like to trek alone. I should say at this point that we are not complete novices when it comes to trekking. We have been walking the Yorkshire Dales and Lake District Hills for many, many years. We have completed all of the 214 Wainwright Hills in the Lake

District. We have also carried our packs across the breadth of England on the Coast to Coast walk. So we are already reasonably fit and we're no strangers to blisters and getting lost in the mountains. Having said that, the Himalayas are a whole new ball game. We needed to up our game to the next level. We started walking with weights in our packs. I filled mine with bottles of water, Deb stuffed her rucksack with mail-order catalogues. Our walks were also made longer and steeper. We were serious about conditioning our bodies to cope with the Himalayan terrain. I was pretty happy with this. It was great to be getting out more and to have a joint purpose and goal in mind.

One of my favourite training hikes that we did, was a wild camp in the Lake District. It was August, and the weather was warm and dry, just perfect for hiking and camping. We gathered together all our gear and divided it up between us. I had 14Kg and Deb had 12Kg. It's about a two-hour drive to get up to the Lake District and we got there about five o'clock in the afternoon. Most walkers were already off the hills and showering ready to go out for the evening. We pulled our packs onto our backs and set off up the hill. These were the heaviest packs we had carried so far and it was a real shock to the system. It was still very warm. Too warm to be carrying a very heavy pack up a very steep hill. However, our mantra was 'no pain, no gain'. After a very hot hour, our mantra had changed to 'What the hell are we doing this for?'. Now the pain of walking up that hill we could cope with, it's just part of being a hill walker. However, the pain I was feeling in my hip, was no joke. It was a deep, nagging pain. This didn't bode well for our Nepal trip. I tried taking some of the weight out of my pack, and it helped. The pain disappeared. Okay, all was not lost. I would have to rethink the contents of the pack I would take on the Annapurna Circuit. If I could trim the weight down to the 10 kg region, I think I could prevent the pain. We found a sheltered spot and began erecting our two-man tent. The sun was just going down and the light across the Lake District hills was just awesome. I don't particularly like using that word. It seems to get used far too frequently and in all the wrong places. But, looking out at the red light accentuating the tops of the mountains near and far, a wonderful panorama of nature at its finest, there was only one word to use 'awesome!'. We rehydrated a packet of chickpea curry and couscous and shared a bottle of wine. After that, we squashed into our two-man tent and dreamt about adventures in the mountains of lands far, far away.

We woke early to another fine August day. The neighbouring hilltops called us to climb them, so we did. Leaving the tent and the rest of our gear behind, while most people were still sleeping, we had a brilliant hike over several hills in the bright morning sunshine. By the time we had packed away and reached the car, I had been converted from a reluctant traveller to an enthusiastic adventurer. Bring it on Nepal. I'm ready for you now.

The following day I laid out all the gear I wanted to carry on the trek. It weighed a whopping 12 Kg. I was determined to get the weight down to 10 kg. So I began to go through each item individually. For each article I asked myself the question 'Is this item essential?'. If the answer was 'No,' it didn't get through and was put to one side. Some items I later came to regret leaving out, such as I only took two pairs of walking socks. That was a mistake. I fully intended to wash a pair out every day, but at higher altitudes, it was much too cold to wash clothes in freezing, cold water, and almost impossible to get them dry if you did. So for several days my socks felt like cardboard and smelled like dead rats. However, I did buy an extra couple of pairs on the circuit. Shower gel was another item to bite the dust. It was too heavy and didn't last long enough. Instead, I took a bar of soap. I still thought this was too heavy, so I cut it in half. This half bar of soap wore out halfway around the circuit, so I ended up using Deb's. Something she wasn't too pleased about. Nonetheless, my pack now weighed in at just under 10 kg.

I don't think anyone likes paying for travel insurance, but if you are hiking the Annapurna Circuit you need it. The place you are most potentially at risk is when going over the high pass of Thorong La. It is at an altitude of 5416 metres, and if you are not properly acclimatised, you run the risk of acute mountain sickness or AMS. This is an extremely serious condition that can cut your adventure short. More importantly, it can cut your life short. There are two types of AMS: HAPE and HACE or High Altitude Pulmonary Edema, and High Altitude Cerebral Edema. HAPE affects the lungs; the lungs fill with fluid, which means oxygen uptake is limited and this will lead to collapse and death. HACE is when fluid builds up in your skull and puts pressure on your brain. It is said it can feel like being drunk; it will be difficult to think logically and judgement is severely impaired. Eventually, it will lead to collapse and death. The best way to avoid AMS is by only increasing your altitude by about 400 metres each day. Also build into your hike a rest day, every four days. Medication is also useful. There is a drug called Diamox. This drug helps your body to acclimatise to the altitude. However, it does come with side effects. It makes you pee a lot and you develop pins and needles in your fingers. But, if it helps to save your life, these small inconveniences are well worth putting up with. If you, or any member of your group, develop symptoms of AMS, you need to lower your altitude as quickly as possible. If the symptoms are mild, going lower down in altitude by 500 metres may be all that is needed. After a day or maybe two days you can resume your trek. On the other hand, if your symptoms are severe, you will need to get down quickly. If a helicopter is needed, it will cost about $10,000, and they won't rescue anyone unless they can pay upfront. It doesn't matter how desperate you are, without the means to pay they will not help you. So you must have good travel insurance. It could save your life. We took out our insurance with the British Mountaineering Club. They do an alpine package that covers you up to 6000 metres.

I read all this information before we travelled and it gave me a few doubts as to whether we were doing the right thing going to the Himalayas. Going on an adventure is one thing, and pushing yourself out of your comfort zone is probably also a good thing, but it's important to be alive at the end of it. I've got more years behind me than I have in front of me, and I am hoping to see my grandchildren grow up before I call it a day. I've seen documentaries on Everest, where those who haven't made it, are just left there on the mountain, frozen and half buried in the snow. Now, I know we aren't going to super high altitudes and spending time in the 'death zone', but I would like to think we would get back home in one piece, as I don't want to die somewhere so far out of my comfort zone that I get left abroad, forever in a foreign land. So, Deb and I came up with a plan. She would look out for me and I would look out for her. We've been together for forty years and it's worked so far, so if it's not broken, don't fix it.

Preparations continued at pace. However, the thing about life is you never know when things might go pear-shaped. And that's just what happened next. My Mum, who is 86 years old, has lived on her own since my Dad died in 2015. I called up most days and took her shopping and did the gardening. She seemed to be getting a little confused, so I called in more often. On this particular day, Deb and I went to her house, but the door was locked. We found her lying on the bedroom floor. It looked like she had fallen out of bed. My heart was in my mouth as I touched her skin. She was still warm, and I tried to wake her. She just moaned. We thought it best to leave her where she was just in case she had broken any bones, so we put a pillow under her head and covered her with a blanket, then rang for an ambulance. They came pretty quickly, and after an initial examination, they thought she might have had a stroke.

We later found out that she hadn't had a stroke, but she had a water infection, which is why she was so confused, more seriously, the fall had resulted in her breaking her pelvis in two places. She was told she would not be able to walk on it for two months. My poor Mum would be in hospital for quite a while. It was now early September. Just over a month before the trip, I wasn't sure if I would be able to go. I went through all the possible scenarios in my head. I even thought one of the kids could maybe have time off work and go with Deb. We had some sleepless nights for a week or two. Mum was moved out of hospital and into a care home for convalescence, and the doctors told us she would probably be there until December. In some ways, this came as a relief, it settled our dilemma. She would be well looked after in the care home, and the rest of the family would call in and make sure she was okay and had everything she needed. We would be back from Nepal by the time she was fit to come home. The adventure was back on track.

We made a list of medications we would need to buy once we got to Kathmandu. There is no need to have a prescription in Nepal just go along to a chemist and ask for what you want. We also made a rough calculation of the amount of cash we would need to take as there would be no ATMs on the trek and lodges don't take cards. YouTube videos were a big help here. There are lots of videos and some of them were very informative, and this gave us a good approximation of the amount of cash we would have to carry with us.

Visits were made to family and friends as we wouldn't see them for six weeks. This was difficult for me as my Mum was in the care home and it felt like I was abandoning her. However, the family rallied around and she was out of danger where she was. Nevertheless, it was hard to say my farewell.

Last-minute instructions were given to our children. We even created a 'doomsday box'; in it were instructions in the event of a disaster and we didn't make it back home. Things like passwords and a quickly put-together last will and testament were in the box. I realise this might seem a little morbid and maybe a bit melodramatic, but it took some of the worry away of leaving family behind. In the event of a disaster happening, and we didn't make it back, at least it would make it that little bit easier for our family to organise things.

It was time to do our final packing. As a couple, we are very different, and this is demonstrated by the contrasting ways in which we approach packing our bags. Whenever we go away on holiday, Deb will do her packing a few days before we're due to go. Then over the next couple of days, she will repack and repack and repack. I pack my bag the day before departure and then leave it, it's done. It's this period, the lull before the storm that unsettles me. I mope around and get frustrated and the anxiety builds up. I am not a natural traveller, and I find the act of getting to destinations very challenging. This trip was no different, in fact, due to the nature of our adventure, and our exotic destination, it was much worse than usual. I was like a coiled spring; I just wanted to be on our way. But, not long to go now.

2

ON OUR WAY AT LAST

The day finally arrived. The adventure was about to begin, and there was no turning back now. Our taxi dropped us off at the railway station in Leeds. We stood in the main concourse surrounded by people rushing about in all directions. Businessmen and women were suited and booted carrying briefcases with mobile phones glued to their ears. Students were hugging and laughing, and just enjoying the experience of being young and alive. Homeless people were being asked to move on by the transport police, not enjoying the experience of being pushed, yet again, from pillar to post. We were early for our train so we stood and watched the world go by, and nobody knew, or could tell, that we were at the very start of our greatest adventure. An adventure that would take us into thin air and into the very heart of the Himalayas where we would walk among giants.

Our train took us right into the centre of Manchester airport where we checked in. It was good to get our luggage stowed away, now we could get a beer and try to relax. We

A Walk Among Giants

have flown lots of times from Manchester and find it a very user-friendly airport. It was going to be a long flight; it was about ten hours to Abu Dhabi with an eight-hour stopover, then another four hours to Kathmandu. The flight to Abu Dhabi was on an Etihad Air Bus. I had never realised just how enormous they are. They appear too big and heavy and look like they could never get off the ground. We've come a long way since the Wright brothers made their maiden flight all those years ago. It was cavernous inside, with row after row of seats. It was the biggest aircraft we had ever flown in.

We settled into the flight. Deb struggled to get her super, sexy flight socks on to prevent deep vein thrombosis, and I found a film to watch. It was a night flight, so at some point the lights were switched off and we tried to get some sleep. At some ungodly hour, we were still awake and needed to stretch our legs, so we went to the back of the plane where there was a small open area in front of the toilets. The advantage of such a large aircraft is there is more space. We did some stretches and then looked out of the small, aircraft window. It was just blackness until occasionally a cluster of lights from a town or city would come into view. We couldn't tell which country we were flying over let alone what towns they were. The people in these places far below were probably tucked up in bed fast asleep and were completely unaware of us high above them, like a small village soaring 600 mph at nearly 7 miles high.

We were pretty tired when we arrived at Abu Dhabi airport, and we still had 8 hours to wait before our next flight. The first hour was okay, and we wandered and explored our way around the large airport. We went into Costa and had a coffee, then we went back to Costa and had another coffee. We started to realise that eight hours is a long time to hang around in an airport. This airport had a long corridor with a view of the runways. It was named the 'library' and had lots of comfortable sofas and coffee tables with a good selection of books available to read while wasting your precious time waiting to fly out of this godforsaken corner of the desert. This seemed like a good place to sit, read or just look out of the window, and maybe nod off for a short while. Having not had much sleep on the plane, we were very tired and soon dozed off. But not for very long. The 'library police' woke us up barking, "No sleeping!" This guy's job was to walk up and down the corridor waking would-be sleepers. I looked at others in the corridor, and most of them had a book open on their lap and their head propped up on their arm trying to give the impression of being awake. We did the same. I wonder what the guy's job title is—Waker-upper, or disturber, or library monitor, or just plain annoying bastard. I think the latter is the most appropriate job title for him. Judging by his smug expression, he enjoyed his job.

We left the library as I needed more coffee. There are pods you can rent where you can lie down and sleep. They reminded me of a TV programme I once watched about Japan. Businessmen would go out on the town to sing karaoke after work, and instead of going home, they would rent pods, or capsules, very similar to these. In the morning they'd go off to work. It's a life, but not one I would fancy, and we didn't fancy the pods either. We found the price of food and drink was extortionate. But theirs was the only show in town, you are in the desert, so where else can you get something to drink? They have you over a barrel, or as we were in the United Arab Emirates, over an oil barrel.

At last, the announcement came for our flight and we

made our way to the gate. We showed our tickets and passports to the ground crew and sat in the waiting area. An elderly German couple sat next to us, but he wasn't happy. He couldn't find his passport. His wife wasn't happy either because he had just shown it to the staff on the desk, and how could he be so stupid to lose it when he had it not more than two minutes ago? My heart went out to the guy. This is the kind of thing that happens to me all the time. We offered to help, and I searched the seating between us and the check-in desk, but I found nothing. The German guy was getting visibly upset and he emptied his rucksack onto the seats. Nothing! This continued for some time until I asked him if he had looked in the lid pocket of his rucksack. He hadn't, and when he opened it up, there it was. The relief on his face said it all. The one thing you do not want to lose when you are travelling is your passport. It could mean being stuck in Abu Dhabi airport indefinitely, and that would be unbearable. My nerves were jangling before this happened, now they were even worse. Even though it wasn't me who had misplaced my passport, it affected my frame of mind. I just wanted everyone to be quiet and sit down. Do not move until we have to board the plane. I am not a relaxed traveller. Once on board, I had a couple of gin and tonics to help calm the nerves and promote an hour's sleep. I could quite easily become alcohol dependent whilst in transit around the world. Maybe that is the answer; I could ask my GP for sedatives and sleep my way to Kathmandu, but not in the Abu Dhabi airport library.

Our second flight was on a smaller aircraft so not quite as comfortable. But it was okay and it wasn't an overly long flight, only four hours. At least we managed to get some sleep without being woken up by the library police. I was feeling anxious about the next step, and hoping it would all go okay. It would be dark when we arrived. I much prefer to get to an unfamiliar place, in the daylight.

We arrived in Kathmandu at about seven in the evening. We weren't expecting to have to queue for an hour to get our visas, so it came as a shock. One thing I have a problem with is queueing. As soon as I see a long queue, I come out in a cold sweat. I had just such a reaction to queueing when the kids were young. It was a Friday and we were going to have fish and chips for our tea. The kids were excited as we didn't have fish and chips very often, but tonight we were. Deb set about preparing for the arrival of the fishy treat; putting the kettle on; warming plates in the oven; laying the table with salt, vinegar and tomato ketchup, not forgetting buttering half a loaf of bread, while I went out in the car, to the chip shop to get them. I arrived at the best chippy in our area to find a queue far too long to get behind. I tried another chippy further down the road. Again the queue was too long. There was nothing else for it, I would just have to resort to going to the chippy with the dubious reputation. When needs must. Would you believe it, the queue here was just as bad. Using the inside of my car as a soundproofed booth, I shouted out at full volume, " What the bloody hell is the matter with everyone? Why can't they make a proper meal instead of coming out for junk food?" Okay, I'll hold my hands up, I'm a hypocrite. My only excuse is frustration induced by severe hunger and my lack of ability to wait in a queue for what would seem like hours of my life. I gave up and headed home. I was a poor excuse for a husband and father. I'm supposed to bring home the bacon, and I couldn't even bring home the fish and chips. While I hung my head in shame, Deb up-cycled the tower of bread and butter into a variety of delicious sandwiches. But it wasn't the same as fish and chips. I'm a bad Dad.

Now Nepal has a population of many Buddhists and Buddhists believe in karma. The episode of the missing fish and chips was my bad karma and it came back to bite me in the backside. There was no getting out of the visa queue, no matter how much I wanted to. On this occasion, it was made much worse because I was imagining our luggage riding around the baggage carousel inviting anyone to walk off with it. All our gear for the trek would be gone in three trips around the carousel and there was absolutely nothing I could do about it. After the longest hour I can remember, we finally got through immigration and could find our bags. They were on a luggage mountain in a corner of the bag reclaim hall; what a relief that was.

We had heard it is best to book a taxi before leaving the airport. It's a little bit more expensive but worth it. The taxi man led us outside to our waiting car. It was complete bedlam outside. There were hundreds of taxis and people offering us everything from porter services to Tiger Balm, but we valiantly resisted their offers with a smile and a polite, "No thank you." We were soon out into the busy roads of Kathmandu City. It was chaotic and noisy with the constant sound of multi-tonal car horns and people driving cars like maniacs. We have been in many big cities and they have all been busy, but this was on another level. It reminded me of the 1980s film 'Blade Runner' with its dystopian streets where everyone was out to get you in one way or another. They might rob you blind or kidnap you and hold you for ransom. Oh God! I hope they don't do that, our kids will never pay to get us back. Well, maybe their Mum, but not me.

I booked our hotel online weeks ago, the Friends Home Hotel in Thamel. This is the tourist district of Kathmandu. Our driver tried, in vain, to persuade us to go to a better hotel that he knew, which was run by his brother-in-law. He also told us it would be better to have a guide and a porter and that he could organise this with a very good company which is cousin owned. He could get us a fantastic discount. I'm sure every word that left his mouth was true, but we weren't going to be distracted; we had a plan and we were going to stick to it. He was very persistent though, and after politely declining his gracious offers many, many times I was relieved to get to our hotel.

Our Hotel looked fine and we were made very welcome; we sat on a comfy sofa in the large foyer and were given a cup of Nepalese tea. This is a heavily, spiced tea and it is delicious. It was the first cup of many we would have on our trek. Nepalese tea became a favourite of ours. We were shown to our room and quickly settled in. But I was restless to get out for a couple of beers to settle my shattered nerves. Hunting the streets for a bar, we negotiated the very dark and intimidating streets of Thamel. The effects of the 2015 earthquake were still very apparent, and as a consequence, there was little or no street lighting. It was a scary place and I feared being robbed by the many groups of shady figures who were hanging around in dark corners and alleyways. My imagination saw danger around every corner. Luckily we soon found a bar. It was the Tom and Jerry Bar. I don't know why I thought this would be a good place for a drink, maybe it was because it was a familiar name in such an alien place. The bar was upstairs, and since it was getting quite late now, it was pretty empty. We sat down and shared a couple of ice-cold bottles of Everest beer. I confided in Deb that Kathmandu scared the life out of me, but she knew me well and had already figured that out. It was a dark and threatening place to be if you didn't know the city well. Deb could tell I was anxious, and she suggested we leave for

Pokhara tomorrow if I thought it was okay. Pokhara is a much more user-friendly place. We could still exchange currency there and get our medications, and permits. She didn't have to ask twice. Let's go to Pokhara, although part of me realised I was running away from my fears, which is never recommended, as it always comes back to bite you in the ass.

Back at the hotel, we organised a tourist bus for early the following morning. There are two types of buses available: the local bus and the tourist bus. The local bus makes many stops and you are likely to be sharing your seat with a goat. However, it's incredibly cheap. We decided to take the tourist bus instead. A little more expensive, but we hoped it would be a more comfortable ride.

After a disturbed sleep, we woke early and had a Nepali breakfast of fried eggs and curried potatoes. We dragged our cases about half a mile down earthquake-damaged streets to the main road where all the buses go. It was pandemonium as we tried to find our bus. We must have been approached to buy Tiger Balm a dozen times while searching desperately for our transport. Maybe they thought these two oldies needed Tiger Balm because they're so decrepit and creaky. I was a nervous wreck again. Planes, trains and automobiles, it doesn't matter which, I get the jitters. To be fair, Deb was not worried, and she took it all in her stride. She is a natural traveller and was far more laid back than I was. We found our bus and took our seats. When we booked the tickets in our hotel, we asked to be on the back seats and this is where we expected to sit, but it doesn't work like that in Nepal. A young lad, who only looked about fourteen, was organising the seating. We just went with the flow. Just like when having work done at the dentist, I kept telling myself it would all be over soon, or in this case, in about six hours.

It took about eight hours, which would be a long stint in the dentist's chair. Off we went. The journey just to get out of Kathmandu City took about two hours. It was chaos. The earthquake damage was everywhere and the whole place resembled a war zone. But we saw kids going to school looking so smart in their clean uniforms, they looked so incongruous to their surroundings. It was like the famous scene from the film Schindler's List, where everything is in black and white except for the little girl in the red coat. Yes, it was definitely like a war zone. Not that I've ever been in a war zone, but I'm pretty sure this is what one would look like. Where there once stood buildings, there were now piles of rubble. Many buildings showed extremely wide cracks in their walls and were held up by wooden supports. It looked like they could collapse at any moment, but people seemed oblivious to the dangers. I suppose if you live here, it is just a fact of life and you have to deal with it.

Our bus rattled along frequently bouncing in and out of deep holes in the road. This could in no way be described as a smooth, comfortable ride. It was more like a theme park ride. On many occasions, to overtake a slow-moving truck, the driver would just pull out into oncoming traffic. It was a white-knuckle ride. We stopped for a lunch break where we had our first dhal bhat. This is a very popular dish in Nepal. It consists of a bowl of lentil soup, rice, vegetable curry, or meat if you prefer, a pickle and a roti. It was delicious. Second helpings are always offered. It is a tasty, hot and very filling meal. The Nepalese have a saying, 'Twenty-four hour, dhal bhat power'. The porters who carry enormous packs up and down impossible gradients, all refuel on large portions of dhal bhat, and if it is good enough for them, it certainly is good enough for us too. We would tuck into many more dhal bhats during our time in Nepal.

A Walk Among Giants

The last hour of the bus journey was physically gruelling. The constant bouncing out of our seats made it difficult to breathe. We kept getting the air knocked out of our lungs and our diaphragms were shot to pieces. After eight hours of being bounced around in the dentist's chair, we finally arrived at the bus station in Pokhara.

3

GETTING TO THE START LINE

It was such a relief to get off the bus. Several taxi drivers approached us for our business. I showed one of them the address of our hotel and off we went. This was a mistake, I made sure never to make again. I didn't ask for a price for the taxi ride. It was a schoolboy error and my inexperience showing. We paid for our expensive ride and went into the hotel. Immediately there was a problem; because we had expected to stay in Kathmandu for two nights, we had arrived in Pokhara a day early. The room I had booked weeks before online was not available until tomorrow. Fortunately, they had a penthouse room available for one night and we could move into our booked room the following day. When I heard the word penthouse, it conjured up visions of opulence and luxury, a room for the filthy rich to enjoy. Well, we looked at the room and to be fair it was great but far from opulent. We took it, and rather than move out to our original room we stayed there for two nights.

The best thing about the room was the view. It had a fantastic roof terrace that overlooked Lakeside, which is the tourist area of Pokhara. But the views we had of the snow-capped mountains of the Annapurna Range were superb. Pokhara is the second largest city in Nepal and it is busy with the hurly-burly you would find in any large city. But the area around Phewa Lake, known as Lakeside, has a very different feel to the place. There are many trekkers here and a fair few hippy characters. There was a constant aroma of marijuana in the air. It was a very chilled-out and laid-back place. Just what I needed to recover from the nerve-jangling few days we had had travelling here.

We spent the next couple of days exchanging currency for Nepalese rupees and obtaining our trekking permits. Because there are no ATMs on the Circuit and lodges don't accept cards, you need to take a large amount of cash with you, which feels very disconcerting. Two different permits are needed for the trek; a permit to enter the Annapurna Sanctuary and a Trekking Information Management System card (TIMS card). This is a card that is shown at various places around the trek and your details are noted in a ledger. If you were unlucky enough to go missing, you would leave behind a paper trail that could be followed up to the last entry into a ledger. Well, that's the theory anyway. Lastly, we called into a pharmacy with our list of medications. The pharmacist was very helpful and gave us advice on if and when to take the various medications. It is so different from England. Doctors are very wary of prescribing antibiotics because it can lead to bacteria becoming resistant to the drugs, and evolving into super-bugs, like MRSA. A person has to be quite ill before they will give you them. Now don't get me wrong, I'm in total agreement that antibiotics shouldn't be given out like smarties. However, in Nepal, and I suspect in most of the world's developing countries, you can just walk into any chemist and buy them over the counter like buying a quarter of wine gums.

Armed with cash, permits and essential medication we headed into town for food. However, we needed to choose a restaurant. I immediately used my phone to access Google and search for the best restaurants to try. After a short while, Deb's patience snapped. 'You always make things complicated. Let's go in here.' She was right. I need to keep things simple.

Another example of making things more complicated than they need to be, happened when Deb and I were in Cambodia visiting our son Tom, who was teaching English in Vietnam. We stayed in a lovely hotel on the outskirts of Siem Riep, called the Indochine Pavillion. Our room was lovely, there was everything you could want. I got up early one morning to use the bathroom, and this is where things went pear-shaped again, all due to me making life too complicated. The lock on the toilet was very elaborate. Why? The toilet was in our room why the hell did it need such an elaborate mechanism? Who the heck was going to come in? I had doubts about how to use it. What would happen if I was in there and got locked in? Think of the shame of locking yourself in the toilet. This has happened to me before; when I was very young I locked myself into a public toilet in Ilkley, and a stranger had to put a penny in to let me out. I couldn't let that kind of thing happen again. So I thought I would test it. I messed around with the mechanism and closed the door. It locked. Aw shit! I was locked out of the toilet. There is only one thing worse than locking yourself in a toilet and that's locking yourself out of the toilet, especially when you need to use it. There was nothing else for it, I had to go down to reception and ask them to open it back up. It was very difficult trying to explain to the young girl in reception, who spoke only a little English, what I had managed to do. I waited in our room until one of the staff turned up with a key and unlocked the door. The Cambodians are very respectful people and the staff of this hotel are even more so. However, I did detect the strain on this young guy's face as he tried to hold back his laughter. Like I said: sometimes I complicate life too much.

After our meal and several beers later we headed back to the 'penthouse' to pack. We had arranged a taxi to drive us to the start of the trek in Besisahar the next morning. A taxi was more expensive than the bus but I couldn't face another white-knuckle, bone-shaking bus ride. So a taxi it was. It had been a relaxing couple of days in Pokhara but now the nerves were back. I had a restless night worrying about what the first day of trekking would bring. Would we manage to find our way? Would we be able to cope carrying our heavy packs in this heat? Would my dodgy hip cope with the constant pressure of trekking? All these doubts and questions were swirling around inside my head, but there was only one way to find out. We just had to get on and do it. Breakfast looked tasty but I couldn't face it. Orange juice and coffee were all I could manage. Pretty stupid really for someone who was going to start a trek carrying a 10 kg pack later that day. Fortunately, I don't smoke or I would have been chain smoking for the last three hours. Deb wanted to wait inside the hotel until the taxi arrived. Being a worry freak, this just wasn't my style. We waited at the hotel gates. I accosted every taxi that pulled up and asked them, "Is this taxi for Oxley?" After half an hour of this, Deb was ready to strangle me. Our taxi pulled up and saved me from a throttling. Off we went leaving my newfound comfort zone of Pokhara behind to head up to the scary foothills of the Annapurna Range.

The taxi driver was an older guy and he seemed to be a very careful driver. This gave us confidence that we would reach our destination in one piece. He pulled into a petrol station on the edge of Pokhara to fill up with fuel. While we were there I noticed two young mechanics burning some rubbish. I couldn't help but think their fire was too close to the petrol pumps. When I fill up in the UK, we have to turn off our lights and keep our mobile phones out of the way. Here they have bonfires on the forecourt. What kind of place had we come to? This dangerous state of affairs brought to mind my very own stupid actions one summer a few years ago.

It was a hot day in July and we thought it would be a good idea to have a barbecue. I had recently bought a new smoker and I was keen to try it out. So I had the idea of smoking some salmon fillets. The smoker uses two meth burners, which heats the wood chips inside the metal box and creates the smoke. The heat also cooks the fish. This is the process of hot smoking, and it produces delicious food. One thing that can be a problem though, is the wind blowing out the flame. So it is best to put the burner somewhere out of the breeze. I had the brilliant idea of putting it in the shed. There wasn't much room in the shed, as it was full of kindling; this abundance of firewood had been produced from old floor boards I had pulled up in our lounge to make way for a new floor. There were about eight large bags full of bone-dry kindling in there. Our camping gear was also stowed away in the shed. This included two large, and full, camping gas cylinders. Yes, you've spotted the stupidity of my smoker idea; the fatal flaw in my plan. But, it is worse than you think. There are two wooden larch lap fences next to the shed, and next to them there are two more large sheds belonging to our neighbours, and I'm sure they also contain flammable items. There had been no rain for about a hundred years and everything was tinder dry. The scene was set for a disaster of monstrous proportions. Why didn't I spot the signs? All went well at first, and I could smell the aroma of smoking hot salmon. I have cooked them before and it is a dish I am quite proud of. Well, we all know pride comes before a fall, and I was about to take a massive tumble. The smell from the smoker changed from delicious salmon to the smell of burning wood. I checked it and noticed the wooden floor of the shed was on fire. I quickly lifted the entire smoker out of the shed. However, some of the remaining meths spilled out and the flames shot up into my face. I lost parts of my eyebrows and burned my hand. I grabbed a sheet we use as a dust sheet when decorating, and tried to smother the fire. The problem was, that the fire had burnt through the floor into the recess under the shed, so it was impossible to starve it of air. Panic set in. I needed help. Like a headless chicken, I tried to explain to Deb what had happened. She didn't realise the seriousness of the situation and began laughing. At times such as this, I seriously question why I married her. I shouted at her "Get some fucking water!" We have a water butt in the garden from which she began to draw water into a bucket. It trickled out like an old guy with a prostate the size of a large orange. I shouted to her to get the hose pipe. I just managed to dampen down the flames in time before they caught the kindling and the gas cylinders. Then, I felt that underrated emotion, of relief. I was shaking like a leaf. If I hadn't got the hose onto the fire when I did, it would have been too big to put out, and too dangerous to try with the gas cylinders ready to explode. It would have spread to the other sheds. I can just imagine the bollocking, and ridicule I would have faced from the fire brigade, and the headlines in the local press: 'Local IDIOT lights BBQ in his shed causing thousands of pounds of damage'. How the hell could I have faced the neighbours after that? Fire and I just don't mix. It is at times like this I can hear my Dad say: "Yer a bloody idiot Dave. When are yer gonna learn?" Sorry, Dad, I'll try to do better next time.

I left the hose spraying water into the shed for two hours to make sure it was completely out. I didn't sleep much that night. I kept thinking the fire had reignited and the hell would start again. Now I am a firm believer in the existence of God. Well, this is a good example of how I believe God works. He will never prevent me from getting into scrapes and doing stupid stuff. He will, however, help me to get out of the troubles I get myself into. He was probably watching me with the smoker and saying to Himself "What the hell is he doing now? Why can't he just do normal stuff?" He's a bit like a dad with superpowers. He wants you to run, and he won't stop you from falling and grazing your knees, but he'll always be there to pick you up when you're bleeding and crying in the dust. God eh, what's He like?

Whenever I mention doing some more smoking, I get a safety talk from Deb. "Don't put it near anything flammable. Don't use too much meths, and don't do it near the house. Scrub that. Just don't use the smoker at all, ever again." She's probably right. Bugger!

PART II

THE TREK BEGINS

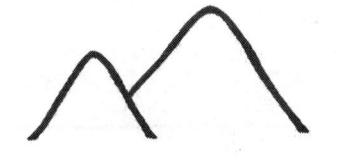

4

ROTTEN RUSSIANS AND A GIANT SPIDER

Three hours after leaving Pokhara we arrived in Besisahar. It was a busy little town. The taxi driver pointed the way to our first stop, which was the tourist police. It's here that you show your permits and a record is taken of your details including your passport number. It had been a long drive and we needed some refreshment before we set off walking, so we called in a small tea room. We both had tea and bought some fruit and orange juice. The young girl looked confused when I paid her. She didn't speak very much English so I hadn't a clue what the problem was. My nerves were getting shredded by now and I just wanted to get on our way. Her mother came out and spoke even less English. However, she took the money I offered and we left. It was only later that I realised I had given them some currency I had left over from Abu Dhabi airport and not Nepalese rupees. I just hope they made a decent profit from my mistake.

It was a hot day and the trail was laid out in front of us. They say the longest journey begins with a single step. This may be true, but our journey started months ago with our surprise retirement gift and only now, at this very instant, are we taking that first step. My emotions were all over the place; relief, fear and excitement in equal quantities. Our bags felt very heavy and the heat was oppressive. After a few days of carrying our heavy packs, they would feel lighter, but for now, it seemed like a massive challenge to carry this weight around the whole circuit. Were we up to it? Are we getting too old to do this? I told myself we are here, and we are going to give it our best shot. We have done tougher things than this before. Okay, that was when we were younger, but experience counts for a lot when you are doing this kind of thing.

This is just what my mind and body had been crying out for; physical activity. Exercise is a great stress buster and my stress needed busting. A quick drink of water, a couple of photos, a sorry from me for being so difficult, a forgiving kiss from Deb, and we were away on an adventure of a lifetime, one we would never, ever forget. We were following directions from the book *Trekking the Annapurna Circuit by Himalayan Travel Guides* which, very importantly, included the new trails that avoided the newly constructed road. The trail began on the dirt road and we soon came to a small village. Here we left the road by crossing over our first suspension bridge to the East side of the Marsyangdi River. Most of the bridges we crossed were modern and appeared to be of a robust and well-built design. We were told engineers from Switzerland had built them, and judging by the sturdiness and quality of their design, I can well believe it. On many occasions, we saw bridges being crossed by dozens of donkeys laden with enormous loads. The combined weight must have added up to many tons so we were confident they weren't going to collapse with our relatively small weight. Once over the bridge, the walking was wonderful;

narrow tracks weaving through golden fields of grain. By now it was early afternoon and getting very hot for walking with a heavy pack. Nevertheless, we had to keep moving as we were hoping to get to Ngadi Bazaar by the end of our first day.

We had a plan that Deb had put together, and at this early stage of the trek we wanted to stick to it. When we came across a shady spot, we would stop and drink some water to try and cool down. Before Ngadi Bazaar was reached, we came to the small settlement of Bhulebhule where we had a late lunch break; Omelette for me and apple pie for Deb. Now it might seem a little strange for a very English pastry like apple pie to be available in the back of Beyond in an exotic place like Nepal. The answer is very simple; the valley we were following has many apple orchards that send their produce to the Kathmandu markets. So if you're an enterprising lodge owner, which they all are, then why not serve trekkers some delicious apple pie? We ate lots of them on the circuit, and they were all different, but they all tasted great with a cup of Himalayan coffee or milk tea.

It was at our lunch stop that we got our first experience of a squat toilet. This was situated at the side of where we, and several other trekkers, were eating. I was desperate so I grabbed our toilet roll, and hid it under my shirt to avoid anyone knowing what I was aiming to do. Feeling more than a little embarrassed, I opened the small, wooden, ill-fitting door which opened with a loud creaking noise. The smell hit me like a slap in the face. I quickly realised that I have zero skills when it comes to using a squat toilet. Also, my body isn't flexible enough to get into a good position to use it accurately. I did my best to squat and take aim hoping that what came out would go down the hole. It was then I noticed that I could see people sitting at their tables. If I could see them, I'm sure if they tried they could see me. Thank God they didn't try. I attempted to be as quiet as I could, which isn't easy when your diet has been vegetable curry for the last week. Finishing this natural and necessary act, I opened the creaky door, and red-faced sat back down. Deb's turn, and she had a similar experience.

Suitably refreshed, and giggling like school kids, we continued to Ngadi Bazaar. After about an hour we came to a small road bridge that crossed a stream. There was a bunch of young kids who came running up to us. They held out their hands and asked for chocolate and sweets. We told them we hadn't got any so they asked for money instead. Now we weren't exactly being mugged, but they were very persistent and weren't taking no for an answer. They reached the bridge before us and stretched a rope across preventing us from getting past. There was no way around the bridge and a battle of wills ensued. If we had some small change, I would have gladly given them it, but our smallest amount was a 500 rupee bill, which is nearly £4, so I didn't feel inclined to give these cheeky little buggers that much cash. Luckily a jeep came up behind us and most of the kids were distracted. I took my chance and lunged forward into the outstretched rope barrier dragging two kids behind me. Thank God they let go, the last thing I needed was to be arrested for child battery. I feel that I must say, at this point, that no child was damaged during this unfortunate incident. Deb thought it was hilarious. I needed a beer.

We arrived at Ngadi Bazaar and booked into the Holiday Trekkers Lodge. I asked the woman in charge "Have you got a room? How much is it? Can we see it? Have you got a hot shower? Have you got WiFi?" We got very used to this routine over the coming weeks, and it served us well. The lodge was a garden lodge; it was very lovely and had an open, grassed area with colourful tin huts around it. We settled quickly into our room and had a much-needed cold beer. This was great. All the months of preparing, training, and all the stress of travelling, but we were here now and doing it. The first day was under our belts and we felt great.

There were two more groups of trekkers staying here. A group of four Germans that were a similar age to us, and we named them the 'Dortmund Four'. The other group was a large group of young Russians. They were loud and brash and we named them the 'Rotten Rowdy Russians'. This is not a slur for all Russians, but this group was Russian and their behaviour was pretty rowdy, and as we found out later, also rotten, so their name was well suited, 'Rotten Rowdy Russians'. We gave most of the trekkers we met nicknames, as it was easier than trying to remember their real names, that's if we ever learned their actual names at all.

After our meal of dhal bhat, we headed off to bed. There was a large net over our double bed, and we assumed it was to keep out the mosquitos. How wrong we were. The nets, as we found out later, were to keep spiders at bay. We didn't see any mosquitos or spiders, but we used the net just in case. We had just started to drop off to sleep when the Russian girls, who were in the room next to ours, started partying as if they were in a club in downtown Moscow. They were drunk and one of them laughed loudly, and constantly, for what seemed like an hour. What the hell was so funny? The girls were all in next to us and the boys were probably acting just as disruptively in another room. After what seemed like a couple of hours, one of the Dortmund Four knocked on their door and asked them to keep the noise down. I applauded his optimism but I don't think the Russian girls were impressed. As the hopeful German was walking away, howls of laughter and banging on the walls emanated from the Russian camp. I felt sorry for our German friend, but I wasn't going to get involved in what could become an international incident. They eventually quietened down, but to say it was a difficult night would be an understatement.

Early the next morning I found I had done another stupid thing; another schoolboy error never to be repeated, and chalked up to experience. If this learning curve gets any steeper, I swear I'll fall down it. I had very foolishly left my boots outside our room when we turned in for the night. Why? I have no idea. They were gone. Blind panic ensued. I was like a man possessed, searching everywhere I could for my boots. There was one thought that I kept coming back to: boots don't walk off by themselves, so someone had moved them. But who would do that? Drunken, Russian girls would move them, that's who. If they had thought it was me complaining about the noise last night, maybe they threw my boots into the Marsyangdi River. My mind was working overtime. I couldn't walk the Circuit in my flip-flops. We would have to return to Besisahar, or maybe go back to Pokhara to buy new boots. Just as my thoughts were turning to despair, the lady who owned the lodge waved me over. She had seen my boots outside our room last night and took them in as it was going to rain. Well, what a way to start the day that was. Okay, things can only get better. And they did get better.

A good breakfast of porridge, fried eggs and chapati and we were off. Day two of our trek and the weather was glorious; the sun was shining and it was bright and fresh; a great day for a long walk. Today we were aiming to get to a village called Jagat. But the first village we would reach would be Bahundanda. This settlement is perched on top of a high

A Walk Among Giants

ridge, so we would have to walk up a steep hillside to get there. But before that, we had to negotiate the building work that was being done on the edge of Ngadi Bazaar. The Chinese are building a series of dams in the river to accommodate several hydroelectric plants. It is a controversial scheme, as it could destroy the natural habitat of many creatures that live in and around the river. Dodging the heavy machinery, we found our way through the construction works, and out of the village.

The building site was now behind us, and we could enjoy the walk to the next village of Bahundanda. It was our first steep hill of the trip, but it wouldn't be the last, that's for sure. In the middle of this village there is an open area, a bit like a village green but without the grass. There was an old Nepalese lady there with the most wrinkled face we have ever seen. Maybe she was only about 40, but she looked 80. She was selling tiny bananas. We bought a bunch from her and sat down to eat them. It was lovely to eat bananas that didn't have thousands of food miles attached to them. She probably picked them that morning right outside her back door. There is also a police check post here where we had to show our permits. While we were resting, and eating our bananas, a group of three young guys also had their permits checked. They looked like they were struggling; their packs looked enormous. We named them the 'Three Amigos'. They poured water over their very hot-looking redheads. We had a quick chat with them before we left them to it and set off again to walk down the other side of the ridge.

The views of the valley below were stunning and we couldn't resist stopping to take photos. The day was getting very hot now as we approached the next village of Ghermu. Just before reaching this village, we had to negotiate a section of the trail that had been carved into a cliff face.

Someone had put railings there to stop daft fools like me from falling down the cliff. These were much appreciated, and we made it safely through in one piece. On reaching Ghermu, we stopped at a lodge and had some lunch. That's one of the great things about this trek, you are never too far from somewhere to eat or stay for the night. This gives you a great deal of flexibility when planning your trek. We ate our lunch of cheese omelette and veg fried rice outside in the shade, all washed down with a flask of black tea. These flasks are a great idea. They come in small, medium and large sizes, are ornately decorated and have a large, cork stopper. Our habit was to get a small flask of tea, which gave both of us three cups. It's very important to keep well hydrated especially once higher altitudes are reached as this aids acclimatisation. A group of six trekkers were also eating there. They had a guide with them and three porters. It was the first large group we had encountered that was being guided and having their bags carried by porters. Now I don't like to judge. No actually, that's a lie; I do like to judge, but I know it's not a good quality and I try my best not to do so. I'm very much a work in progress. The group were Americans and judging by their expensive gear, they were rich Americans. I said to Deb, with my judgemental hat on, "These rich plonkers are going to buy their way around the Circuit, and where's the sense of achievement in that?" Deb gave me one of her looks; the look that meant I had gone too far. She was right. I didn't know anything about these people. I wound my neck in. I made a mental note to myself; live and let live everyone is different, and everyone has their reasons for being here and doing this trek. But, I am so glad that we did the trek unguided and carrying our own gear. You could say I am very proud of us for doing it unaided. But then we have always been an independent couple.

I never felt like trekking after a large lunch, but we still had a fair way to go before we reached Jagat, so on we went. The path led steeply down to the river where we crossed a long suspension bridge to the small settlement of Syange. This led to the jeep road. There was no way of avoiding this section of road, so we put our heads down and plodded on. Some walkers stay on the road most of the time. I'm not sure why, as many new trails and tracks are being made to avoid the road. The term road is a very loose term for what in reality is a very rough, dirt track; there are deep holes and large, loose rocks everywhere. This is fine for large trucks, jeeps and off-road vehicles but not your average Ford Focus. In the dryer seasons, as it is now, the dust swirls around on the road and gets everywhere. If a jeep or truck came past while you were on the road, the dust would be quite overwhelming. A hat, glasses and tight buff are absolute essentials. Maybe some stay on the road because they don't know about the new trails. Maybe some feel safer because it's harder to get lost on the road, and it can be quicker. We found that a lot of the larger, guided groups stuck to the road. Could this have been because it's faster and the guide could lead more groups during the trekking season, and hence make more money? Am I being cynical? No, I don't think I am. We met some guides who were trying to give their groups a full experience and were very proud to show off their beautiful country. On the other hand, it was obvious that not all guides were cut from the same cloth, and you would see trekkers struggling along the hot, noisy, dusty road when they could have been enjoying the quiet, lovely tracks that weaved around fields of grain and through old, beautiful villages and settlements. This is the real Nepal, and it's not to be missed. That's one of the advantages of being self-guided and travelling independently, you go where you want to go and not where the guide wants to go.

To enter the village of Jagat, we had to climb a short, steep hill. Coming up behind us was a motorbike. He shot past us which was no mean feat on this bumpy road. On turning through one of the many zig-zags, we saw the bike rider up ahead. He had stopped and got off his bike. I got the feeling he was waiting for us. I felt very vulnerable and I could feel adrenaline speeding up my heart. We were in a strange unfamiliar country; it was at the very beginning of our trek, so we were carrying a very large amount of cash, which the motorbike guy would have known, and there was no one else around. We had one thing in our favour though, we had our trekking poles, and I quickly formulated where I would strike him if it came to a fight. Now I know this might seem like an overreaction, but it is my job to keep my wife safe and if this had happened in some of the areas where we live in Leeds, I would be worried. We walked up to him and he said, "Namaste, hello how are you?" Now I know should never judge a book by its cover, but I believe you can tell a lot about a person from their face, and this guy had a good face. My adrenaline started to subside, and my heart rate returned to normal. We chatted for about five minutes. He asked us about which country we were from, if we had children, what jobs we did. He even asked our age and was impressed that we were carrying our own bags. I'm not sure this was a compliment though; we're not that ancient. We had many conversations just like this during our stay in Nepal. The Nepalese are very friendly and they love to practice their English language skills. He said goodbye and tried to set off on his bike. Because the road was so steep, and the surface so loose, he couldn't get enough traction, so we gave him a push. Another lesson learnt on my steep learning curve. Try to be more trusting, think better of people, and give people the benefit of the doubt when possible.

Going through the village we saw the strangest sight; a woman was squatting on top of a great pile of small stones. She had a large rock at her feet and was hitting it with a hammer and chisel. We could only assume she was making stone chips to be used in construction. Maybe it was for her own use, or maybe she sold them, but what a hard way to make a living, and how long had it taken her to make that pile of stones? We have to keep reminding ourselves that Nepal is a very poor country, and some people Nepalese are very poor indeed. By comparison, we are very, very rich, and very, very lucky. They are also the kindest and happiest people we have ever met.

We booked into the 'Mont Blanc Lodge'. It seemed a little strange that a lodge in the Himalayas would be named after a mountain in the French Alps, but it looked clean and welcoming, so why not? Our room was on the second floor up some very steep steps, that were more like a ladder. After we had unpacked, we had a beer in the outside dining area and chatted with the owner. He spoke excellent English and asked us about our lives in England, and we asked him about what we could expect from the rest of our trip. When we told him we were from Leeds, he wanted to know all about Leeds United football team and the games we had been to. He seemed genuinely disappointed when he discovered that we weren't football fans. Other trekkers soon turned up and we all sat together outside, all excited at the prospect of the adventure in front of us. We ate our evening meal and chatted some more with our Nepalese host.

It had been a long, tough day, and we had hiked for eight hours and were now full of dhal bhat and beer, a combination guaranteed to induce sleep. It was time for bed. We very carefully negotiated the ladder to our room and turned on the light. Deb let out a terrifying scream. Now we've been together a long time and I knew exactly what that scream meant: spider! It was high on the wall and like no spider I had ever seen before It must have been ten centimetres across with thick legs, but it was its striking colour that I found most unsettling: bright green, light brown and orange. At home, I am the spider catcher, and I use a pint glass which I put over the spider and slip an envelope underneath it. Then I have to take it outside and let it go, and tell it not to come back and tell all its friends the same. Now I know this is bizarre, but it is a ritual that Debbie made me do many years ago and it is now firmly engrained into my psyche. I am sure our next-door neighbour thinks I am quite insane, and he might have a point. Looking at this giant spider on the wall, I don't think a pint glass would be big enough, and I don't think it would take kindly to me telling it what to do. I considered hitting it with my boot, but what kind of mess would it make, its big, round, hairy body was huge, and I'm sure it would have been stuffed with disgusting innards. In this hiatus, I thought I would take a photo of the beast. Whilst fumbling for my camera Deb screamed again. I looked up and the spider was gone. It had travelled at the speed of light through one of the many gaps between the wall and the ceiling. It's the speed of a spider that freaks Deb out. Now we had an issue; we couldn't sleep knowing the monster could come back, and maybe crawl into our sleeping bags with us. What to do? Well, we did two things; we moved our beds away from the walls and left the light on all night hoping the brightness would deter it from coming in. It was a long night, but we survived. This wasn't to be our only encounter with spiders on our trek

5

THE THREE AMIGOS AND POLICE PATROLS

Our bags packed and ready, we started our third day of the trek. Today we were hoping to trek through Chamje and Tal to reach Dharapani. We always start our day by reading the guidebook, and it looks like it's going to be a long day with lots of uphill; however, there is only a short section of about half an hour that we will be walking on the road. Deb has started with a cold, so if it gets worse, we have the option of cutting the day short and staying at Tal. Leaving Jagat, and the spider behind, we followed the road out of the village. A short while later we saw the red and white painted stripes that indicated where we left the road and followed the path. When in doubt, we follow these markers. The path we took climbed steeply upwards through a lush green forest. This got the heart pumping. At the top of the path was a wonderful lodge called The Rainbow Waterfall Hotel. From here we got a fantastic view of a large waterfall on the opposite side of the river.

An hour later we were back on the road. It would have been much quicker to stay on the road from Jagat, but we wouldn't have experienced that wonderful forest and the view from the top. It was only a short section of road that led us to Chamje, and from there we crossed over a suspension bridge to the east side of the river, which we called the good side because it was off the road, and at this time of day, it was in the shade. We were very grateful for the shade as we were hiking up pretty steeply again. It was here I got my one, and only, blister of the trek. I couldn't understand it, my boots were well broken in and I don't usually have problems with blisters. I took my boot off and it felt tight, I realised my feet had swollen and made my boots feel tighter. I applied a blister pad from our first aid box and loosened off my laces. Why did my feet swell? Maybe they were still swollen from the long flights, or maybe it was the heat? I have no idea, but Deb was pleased she had got to use our first aid box. She has been carrying her 'box of tricks' for years. Whenever we go hiking she always carries it in her bag, so this was a special moment when she actually got to use it. Whatever floats your boat.

At the top of the hill was a tea shack with a long table in the shade. We took our packs off and enjoyed a lemon, honey and ginger tea, and it was so refreshing. We sat there for a good thirty minutes cooling down in the breeze and looking at the fantastic view of the amazing Marsyangdi Valley. This felt like heaven, and exactly why we came to Nepal. This moment would stay with me long after we had returned home, a moment that would live with me for the rest of my life.

The trek from here levelled out and a great river basin opened up. We could see Tal in the distance and the prospect of a good lunch spurred us on. Deb was still feeling under the weather, so a rest with a good meal would do her good. Tal is a lovely village with colourful lodges on each side of the main street. The road doesn't go through the village so there is a very peaceful atmosphere; all the lodges were so beautiful and had gardens full of bright flowers. We chose our lodge and ordered lunch. We both went for the veg momos. Along with dhal bhat, momos are a Nepalese speciality. They are dumplings filled with veg, or meat if you prefer, and can be steamed or fried. I prefer the fried variety and dip them in ketchup or hot chilli sauce. We are learning that when lunch is ordered you have to be patient, and just take the time to rest and enjoy your surroundings. This is because all the food is made freshly to order. We went into the kitchen to see our momos being prepared, and the lady was squatting on the floor with a small, wooden table only a few inches off the ground. She rolled out the dough with a very thin wooden roller, then she used a cutter to make circles. She put some of the veg filling in the middle of each circle, and very skilfully folded it into a crescent shape, making the whole process look so easy. After that, she dropped them into hot oil to fry. They tasted delicious.

The walk from Tal was so beautiful, as the path clung closely to the side of the hill. This part of the valley is narrow and the sides are very steep. The road on the other side of the valley had been cut into the rocks and we watched in amusement at the groups walking along dodging the jeeps and trucks. Our path took us quite high up and then we plunged back to the river before crossing a suspension bridge just before we came to the village of Dharapani. That's the thing about this trek, most of the villages are on the side of the valley where the new road goes. So we were constantly crossing the river to do our trekking, and crossing back to use the lodges. On crossing this bridge, we bumped into the Three Amigos again. They looked even more knackered now than when we met them at Bahundanda. We said our hellos and then entered the village. The houses and shops were spread out for a good half a mile along the dirt road. We found a lodge and checked in. It was the 'New Tibetan Hotel'. It had been eight hours since we had set off from Jagat, and we needed a cold drink, so we sat outside and shared a bottle of cold Everest beer. I say we shared, but in truth, I drank most of it.

Time for a shower. I asked the owner where the shower was and he went off to get the key. It did beg the question, why does the shower need to be locked? After unlocking the door he showed me how to use it. The gas-powered shower was loosely attached to the wall and looked ancient. My hopes of having a hot shower slowly drained away like soap suds down the plug hole. He gave me strict instructions not to turn the heat dial up from where it was currently set. I knew from this that it was going to be a lukewarm shower at best. The shower walls were bare stone and there was a window at the far end. However, there was no glass in the window and the wind blew straight against my now cold, naked body. I turned the shower on and waited for some warmth. After what seemed like an age, the temperature of the water increased by a few degrees. There was nothing else for it, I forced myself under the stream of tepid liquid. There was a worrying smell of fumes and propane gas so I certainly was not going to disobey the strict instruction not to touch the controls. I have a poor track record when it comes to safety and devices that produce heat, so I left it well alone. Needless to say, it was a very quick shower and then out. Debbie decided wisely to give it a miss.

We ordered food for six o'clock, so with over an hour to kill, we went out and explored the village. We bought some Snickers and more toilet rolls. We ate a lot of Snickers on the trek; it was our go-to chocolatey treat, and always gave us a burst of much-needed energy. We had earlier noticed a German bakery and went to check it out. You might ask what is a German bakery doing in the middle of the Himalayas? I have no idea, but lots of the larger villages had German bakeries, which we always found amusing when you consider we are in the back of beyond in Nepal, but they were always a very welcome sight. The Three Amigos had the same idea as ourselves and were sat outside the bakery drinking coffee and smoking cigarettes. We ordered some drinks and sat down with them. They said they couldn't believe how fast we trekked past them earlier. I explained that our packs only weighed ten kilos, whereas their packs looked much heavier. We couldn't believe it when they told us they were carrying 25 kilos each, no wonder they always looked knackered. "What the hell have you got in them?" I asked. "All the essentials that we might need for our trek," came the indignant reply. I realised I might have come across as a little condescending, so I diffused the situation by politely asking what they were using to sterilise their water. This was the key to gaining their trust. These three were 'gadget men' and loved to explain how their equipment worked. And they did have a lot of equipment. They were carrying every gadget known to man; they had a satellite phone, just in case they got into trouble going over Thorong La; they had several different water purifying gadgets; however, most incredibly, they were carrying a tent each, just in case the lodges were full. They also had cooking stoves, and all the rest of the camping gear they thought they might need. Why? If the lodges were full, you could still get food there and if they didn't have a room, you would be welcome to sleep in the dining room; this is where the porters sleep all around the Circuit. Now I've heard of taking precautions and having a belt-and-braces attitude, but this was taking it way too far. One of the lads showed us his sore shoulders where the straps of his bag had rubbed away at his skin. How could you possibly enjoy the experience of trekking in this wonderful country, when every energy-sapping step was slowly but surely producing painful, angry welts over large areas of your upper body? Every day must have been like running a marathon wearing a suit of sandpaper. I got the feeling they thought of the trek as a challenge to be conquered, rather than something to be enjoyed. Ah well, one man's meat is another man's poison, and I think if I had been carrying that kind of weight it would have poisoned me after the first day, still they were good lads and so we wished them good luck on the rest of the trip.

Back to our lodge for tea. Now the shower might have been dodgy, but the food was excellent. However, after the pastry I had eaten in the bakery, I couldn't manage the usual second helpings. The evenings were becoming quite cold, and after a day's trekking, we were ready for an early night. Our room looked over the river, where the water was flowing quickly over the rocks, so we fell asleep in our sleeping bags with the sound of the river below.

We woke early and packed our bags, then down for a breakfast of apple porridge and omelette with chapattis. We needed a good breakfast this morning as this was going to be a tough day. Dharapani is at an altitude of 1860 metres, and we were walking to Chame with an altitude of 2670 meters, which is an elevation gain of 810 metres. That's a lot of height gain in one go. If we were higher up the circuit, it would be too much height gain to do in a day, but because we were still under 3000 metres it should be okay. It would be tough, but it would also be safe, although I was still concerned about Deb, as her cold seemed to be getting worse. We crossed the suspension bridge over to the east side of the river and made our way along the track. It was very steep, narrow and overgrown, so much so that we started to doubt we were on the right track. I think the track was little used because there was also a new track on the west side of the river which climbed high above the road. The track might have been a hard one, but I'm so glad we took it, we walked past houses that looked a thousand years old and through fields being ploughed using oxen to pull the plough. Nothing had changed here for hundreds, or maybe thousands of years, apart from brightly coloured trekkers like us walking past. We crossed back over the river at Danaqyu and replenished our water bottles. It was busy with a few large groups of trekkers, so we sat outside one of the lodges in the sunshine, and ordered some lemon, ginger and honey tea, and watched the world go by for half an hour.

Our next stop would be Temang, a 350-metre ascent through a lovely woodland setting. It was hard going, but at least we were in the shade most of the time. One of the large groups was just ahead of us. Most of the trekkers were just carrying a small day pack, as their porters were carrying the bulk of their luggage. I say most, because the trekker in front wasn't carrying anything at all, and then he did something that annoyed me. He took off his jumper, and rather than carry it, he gave it to a porter to carry. This made my blood boil; these porters were carrying very heavy loads, over 40 kilograms, and this arrogant dickhead was treating them like slaves. I mean, for the love of God, I'm sure he could have managed to carry his own bloody jumper. He was a knob-head with little or no moral fibre. I know he might say it's what they get paid for, and this is true, but they should be shown respect and gratitude for the job they do. I hope he tipped them well at the end of his trek, but, somehow I doubt very much that he did.

Temang is situated on the top of a hill and as we reached it, I wasn't feeling too good. I had a headache and I felt sick. These are early signs of altitude sickness. This surprised us both as we were still under 3000 meters. If it was due to getting too high too fast, it was only mild, and Deb said she would keep a close eye on me, so no change there then. But, it's funny how doubts can creep in; we're only at an altitude of around 3000 metres and Thorong La is at 5416 metres. Would this be too high for me? Everyone is different and there is no way to tell how well a person will adapt and deal with high altitude. Fitness has nothing to do with it, and there is no way of knowing who will cope with the thinning air. Only time would tell, so I kept my doubts to myself.

We had a drink at Temang but I felt too nauseous to eat anything, so we carried on. The trail levelled off now and the walking was easier. At the next village, which was called Thanchouk, we had a stop and something to eat. We tried Tibetan bread and homemade jam. Although I was still feeling sick, I fancied something sweet to eat. The Tibetan bread was round and flat with three slits cut into it. It had been fried and was hot and crispy. I broke a piece off and scooped some jam onto it. Nepali food never disappoints, it was just what I needed, and set us up for the last leg of our day's walk to Chame.

We arrived in Chame at about 3 o'clock and looked for a lodge to stay in. We chose the Tilicho Lodge. The lodge owner was a young woman and she showed us to our room; we followed her outside and up a set of wooden steps, then we weaved through a maze of small corridors to emerge at the back of the lodge where she gave us the key to a small, chalet-style room, a little like a beach hut painted bright pink. It wouldn't have looked out of place on the seafront at Whitby. It was lovely; the inside was lined with pine planks and the single beds had thick blankets on. The shower was just outside our chalet and she said it was a hot shower. She lied! Our room was great, but the shower was not hot. It was freezing, so I made do with what we used to call a 'lick and a flick' or a rub down with a cold flannel. We ordered our evening dhal bhat and went for a walk in the village. There were quite a few shops, so I bought a couple of pairs of walking socks and some coconut biscuits. We noticed there was a chemist so Deb asked for something for her cold, and was given Sinex tablets. Hopefully, these would do the trick, as her cold was becoming worse.

There is a police station at Chame and we saw a group of police doing a training run through the village. There were about thirty of them and they were all dressed in smart, dark blue uniforms and they carried rifles in front of them. When they finished their run, they entered a heavily guarded compound with a high fence topped with barbed wire. This seemed strange to us, as Chame is a small village in a very rural area. Why on earth would they need such a high police presence? We began to learn more about the recent history of Nepal throughout our trek. In a very small nutshell, a ten-year civil war began in 1996 when the Nepalese Communist Party, known as Maoist rebels, rebelled against the Parliamentary Monarchy in an attempt to form a People's Democratic Republic. The civil war ended in 2006, with about 19,000 people killed, when a peace agreement was signed between the Maoists and the Seven Party Alliance. Since then governments have come and gone in quick succession. So it seems that Nepal is a politically unstable place, hence the full-on police presence, due to nervous politicians, even in rural Nepal.

Back at the lodge, we had a hot meal then off to our sleeping bags to keep warm. I was really glad we had invested in good sleeping bags. We choose Rab Ascent sleeping bags. They were expensive, but they were worth every penny. In the old days, my sleeping bag was the cheapest I could find, and it didn't keep the cold out, or with my physicist hat on, I should I say, didn't keep the heat in. When I was about 18 years old, my friends and I regularly slept rough in our cheap sleeping bags in Scarborough. We would catch the train from Leeds and have two or three days enjoying the pubs and trying, in vain, to chat up girls. We couldn't afford a bed and breakfast place, even if one would have had us, which I seriously doubt they would. Instead, we would take our sleeping bags and sleep by the castle walls. By sheer fluke, we came across a secluded grassy area to sleep on. Until then we used to sleep on the steep slopes of the castle away from prying eyes. However, one night we were in our sleeping bags when we were woken up by a guy walking his dog. It was pitch black so we never saw his face. All we saw was his cigarette glowing every time he took a puff. He told us he knew a way over the castle walls and he and his mates go in on a night with their dogs to hunt rabbits. He also said we were in a dodgy place to sleep, as his mates would soon be coming this way and their dogs would probably have a go at us. He told us of an ideal place to bed down and described directions to the secret patch of grass actually on top of the castle walls. After he had left, we went to find the secret sleeping place, and to our astonishment we found it. If you didn't know it was there, you would never see it. We had to climb part of the castle wall, but instead of looking down over a sheer drop into the town, we found ourselves on a grass platform big enough to fit about five sleeping bags. This became our go-to place to sleep rough when we were in Scarborough. Our parents thought we were crazy roughing it, but these were unforgettable days; it was freedom, laying there looking up at the stars with our whole lives in front of us. We were fit and strong and had no ties or responsibilities, absolutely free at the start of our adult lives, although our parents didn't think we were behaving like adults. My God, I even had hair back then. But I wouldn't want to go back to those days even if I could. That must be a sign I've done something right along the way, don't you think? So the Rab sleeping bags turned out to be a wise investment. The lodges also supplied blankets, and if the mattress was particularly hard, I would fold the blanket and lay on it to give me a softer bed.

Apart from Deb's cold, and my altitude-induced nausea, I thought we were doing pretty well. We had been trekking for four days, and I felt we were walking into fitness; our bags didn't feel as heavy as they did at the start; we hadn't lost our way, and our plan was still intact. However, the most important thing was we were enjoying the trek, and we were keen to get up early in the morning to walk another day. It felt great to be sharing an adventure with my Deb, both seeing and experiencing the same wonderful sights and sounds.

6

TROUBLE WITH DOGS

Day five of our trek was to Upper Pisang at an altitude of 3350 metres, so that's a height gain of 640 metres, with a tough hill to climb. Upper Pisang is the start of the upper part of the Manang area. For us, it meant no more alcohol until after Thorong La as alcohol can work against the acclimatisation process. It also marks the point we started to take Diamox, the drug that helps the body to acclimatise.

On leaving Chame that morning, we were accosted by a large group of aggressive, barking dogs. I could feel the hairs on the back of my neck starting to rise. I'm glad we were walking with our trekking poles, and we used them to fend them off. We weren't sure why they were barking at us, but they seemed pretty annoyed about something, which is unusual as most of the dogs we have come across on our trek have been friendly. One of the lodge owners heard the commotion and came out and dispersed the pack, allowing us to continue on our way.

I like dogs, and they don't scare me, but this has not

always been the case; when I was very young, I was terrified of them. There was one dog in particular that gave me nightmares, and it regularly walked along our street. This was in the days when people used to let their dogs roam around free. It was a large, white dog; some said it was an albino German Shepherd, while others said it was a Pyrenean Mountain dog. All I knew was it was twice my size and it scared the crap out of me. On one fateful occasion, I was playing on my tricycle just outside of our gate, when it came onto the street. It was on the other side of the road, and to be fair to the dog it was just walking past and minding its own business, it probably didn't even notice me. My reaction, or should I say my overreaction, was to lean so far over on my trike that I fell off. When I say fell off, I really mean I FELL OFF. I hit the pavement face first, knocking my front teeth out and making a bloody mess on the pavement. I screamed loud enough to wake the dead. My mum came rushing out, along with the neighbours, to find me crying in a pool of blood and bits of my teeth. Okay, it looked bad, but kids are resilient and once I was cleaned up I was okay. The lost teeth were part of my milk teeth so no great loss.

Now you would think I would have learned from this experience, after all, that the dog was not aggressive, and I could have carried on playing and come to no harm whatsoever. But, some weeks later the same thing happened again, I face-planted onto the pavement at the mere sight of the dog. The only difference this time was, that there was less blood and no teeth, as there was only a wide gap where my teeth used to be.

Years passed by and my parents were concerned that my front adult teeth were not growing. They were nowhere to be seen. So off we went to visit the dentist, who sent us off to the dental school in Leeds for an X-ray. The X-ray showed that my front teeth were growing just fine, but not into my mouth, they were growing into my palate instead, and I would need surgery to sort it out.

The day of the operation arrived and my Dad drove me to the hospital. I was only about nine or ten so I didn't understand what was going on, but when my Mum waved us off at the gate, and she was crying, that got me scared. My next memory was waking up on a hospital bed after the operation. I remember my pillow was cold, wet and sticky with saliva and blood. My Dad came in to see me and I tried to look up at him but one of my eyes was stinging. Each time I looked at the bright light my eye watered badly and it stung painfully. The surgeon told my Dad that something may have been spilt into my eye during the operation. Like What? What were the surgeons doing, having a fucking party? Maybe they spilt a pina colada in my eye or perhaps a rogue pork scratching. What they spilled into my eye I will never know. Now, remember this was the sixties, and people didn't sue doctors or the NHS in those days. If it happened now, I am sure we would have had a solicitor and a legal team to handle our negligence claim. We may have been able to check security cameras and catch the negligent bastards partying; dancing on the operating table clumsily spilling cocktails and scattering nachos, while I'm laid there unconsciously unaware of the drunken surgeons dancing on my limp and helpless body, catching tab ends and cheese and onion crisps in my bloody eyeball. But, it was a different world then.

I was taken in a wheelchair down to the ear, nose and throat department where I had my eye rinsed out. This was a weird experience, I'm not sure how they did it, but somehow they popped my eye out and rested it on my cheek. It was still attached to my head, but I had no control over it at all. From a large jug, they poured warm water over my eye, and I could see the water falling on it, but I couldn't blink or close my eye because my eyelids were no longer covering it. When they rotated my eye I could see the rest of the room, all without any input from me whatsoever. They then popped my eye back in stuck a bandage over it, and sent me home. They told my parents to keep me inside for a month with the curtains drawn, as I had to keep out of bright light.

Now, they say every cloud has a silver lining, and the upside to this is, that I got out of school for a month and my aunts and uncle regularly came around and brought me sweets and comics. The downside was, I couldn't play out with my mates and I was desperate to tell them about having my eye out.

Shortly after this, my Dad got us a dog. He was called Patch, and I loved him. That did the trick, and my fear of dogs was gone forever. Anyway, that was a lifetime ago, and we still had a long walk in front of us.

We climbed up through pine forests, which reminded us of walking in Mallorca. If you have never been walking in Mallorca, you are missing a treat. Mallorca is not all beaches, lager louts and foam parties. Go to the north-west of the island where a mountain range called the Sierra de Tramontana is located, and there you will find some of the best mountain walking in Europe. These are limestone mountains with well-worn tracks going through pine woods and hillsides full of holme oak trees, with wild rosemary lining the way. The area is covered in olive groves and fields full of lemons and oranges. The mountains are quite high with many going over the 1000 metre mark. Wild goats roam the hillsides and black vultures can be seen soaring high above. We have been going there for many years, and God willing, we will go back many more times.

But that's another trek on another continent, and we were in Nepal. After a couple of hours walking, we came to the outskirts of the settlement of Bhratang, where we were surrounded by apple trees; thousands of them all behind high fences with lots of warnings to keep out. This guy wasn't messing about, he was serious about his apples and didn't want anybody stealing them. Our guidebook told us that the owner had imported a staggering 60,000 apple trees from Italy, making it the largest apple farm in Nepal. He was also building a very large luxury lodge. This would be interesting to see; we just couldn't imagine anything luxurious on the Circuit. Arriving at Bhratang we saw the luxury lodge, and it wouldn't have looked out of place in an upmarket ski resort in Switzerland, but it did look very out of place here in rural Nepal. There must be money to be made in apples, no wonder he can afford his posh new pad. Opposite the new lodge was a group of old buildings where apples were being loaded onto trucks. There was a cafe there, so we called in and bought some tea and apple muffins. We ate them outside in the sunshine and watched as thousands of apples were being loaded onto the waiting trucks. We bought a couple for later in the day and continued along the road.

Shortly after leaving Bhratang, we came to a section of the road that had been hewn out of a vertical cliff face and we couldn't resist taking some photos. We had to be careful though, when a jeep came along the road we made sure we were against the cliff wall and not the cliff edge, it was a long drop down into the river.

A Walk Among Giants

The walking here was just fantastic and we were both in good spirits. We soon came to an amazing natural rock formation called Paungda Danda, also known as Swarga Dwari, which translates as 'Gateway to Heaven'. It is a very high wall of rock that curves around the valley in one continuous slab; it is very striking because it is so vast and completely smooth, certainly not a sight you see every day. Local Buddhists believe the spirits of the dead must ascend its high, smooth wall to reach heaven. No spirits were ascending when we walked past, or if there were, they must have been invisible spirits; however, we did see several grave markers along the trail, as this is seen as an auspicious place to be buried. I could think of worse places to spend eternity, but, unlike the dead, we couldn't linger as time was rolling on and we were ready for lunch. All this walking sharpens the appetite.

We crossed the river on yet another suspension bridge and then climbed steeply up through a dense forest. At the side of the track were some stalls selling food and drink and also the ubiquitous jewellery. I'm a sucker for bracelets and the bright, blue beads attracted me like a magpie, I think it's a throwback to when I went through a hippy phase as a teenager. Whenever I smell goats it reminds me of my old Afghan coat, which had a unique smell of a blend of goats and cheese. Some might say, as my Mum frequently did, that it smelled of sweaty socks. No wonder I found it so hard to get girlfriends. I slipped the turquoise bracelet on and bought a couple of hard-boiled eggs to keep me going at lunchtime, and we sat down to eat them. A very kind Spanish girl asked if I would like some salt and pepper for my eggs, and from her bag, she produced two tiny silver foil packets. It was only a bit of salt but it was very kind of her. The Spanish are such friendly people, and eggs need salt like people need friends. The eggs tasted great.

The path levelled out at the top of the hill, and an hour later we reached the small village of Dhukur Pokhari. We looked for a lodge with tables in the sun and ordered some tea and Tibetan bread. It was a short break as we were both conscious of the time and we were eager to reach Pisang. As we left Dhukur Pokhari, there was a fork in the road. The vehicle track went off to the left and down to Lower Pisang, and the path to the right went up to Upper Pisang. The path to Upper Pisang is also known as the high route and has two advantages: the views and scenery are spectacular and because you spend longer at a higher altitude it is better for acclimatisation. We, of course, took the high route to Upper Pisang. The path crossed the river and rose gently upwards. We were feeling the effect of the thin air now. My brain told me that this path was not very steep and I could walk it quickly, but when I tried, I soon became out of breath. My brain told me one thing and my body told me something different. The rarefied air had rendered me unsynchronised.

The village of Upper Pisang was amazing, as it was built into the rocky hillside. We navigated our way through its steep paths between several lodges until one took our eye. It was right at the top of the village. It looked down over the valley and we couldn't believe the view, Annapurna's snow-capped peaks right in front of us, it took our breath away.

We were told by the lodge owner that they didn't have a hot shower, but they could provide us with a bucket of hot water. We have been disappointed by most of the showers so far, so we thought we would give it a try. The owner's daughter put the biggest kettle I have ever seen on the kitchen stove while we had a cup of masala tea. The kitchens in these lodges are amazing, basically just a wood-burning stove with a hot plate on top, but somehow they manage to produce dozens of different meals with apparent ease. It was wonderful to see them working with the light from the flames lighting up their faces and smoke filling the room.

Half an hour later our bucket was ready. We took it into where the cold shower was housed, which was typically a concrete floor with a glassless window where the cold wind could blow in. We stripped off quickly, as we realised this was best done as fast as we could before we froze. Having a shower, or even a hot bucket, with your partner, should be a sexy thing to do, but this was not the case. Any thoughts on that subject were soon quashed by the cold wind and the less-than-luxurious surroundings. It was funny though, and we laughed our way through it, taking turns to put our cold feet fully into the bucket. This was our only experience of a hot bucket on the Circuit, which was a shame, as it was much warmer and more fun than the showers we had encountered.

We dressed in our warmest clothes and had a walk to the new Buddhist Gompa that was being built at the top of the hill. Neither of us had ever been inside a Gompa before. The sign said, 'Take off your shoes before entering,' so we took our boots off and went inside. The first thing we noticed was the powerful smell of incense. The second thing was the colours, it has got to be the most colourful place of worship we have ever been in. The Church of England could learn a thing or two from the decor of these buildings, it was just stunning. We didn't understand the significance of many of the religious objects inside, but the feeling of reverence was tangible, and we both felt a sense of the importance of Buddhism to the Nepali people we had met on the trek. However, Buddhism is not the major religion in

Nepal, approximately 80% of Nepalese are Hindus, but in certain areas, such as the Menang Valley, Buddhism is very prevalent. This is a very simplistic view of the religions of Nepal, as there are many other religions, but the numerous Buddhist Mani walls and prayer wheels are an indication that Buddhism is the main religion on this side of Thorong La.

After our evening meal, yes dhal bhat again, we chatted to a young French couple. They were quite young, maybe early twenties and were trekking with a guide. They asked us about an item on the menu they didn't understand; it was custard. He had never encountered custard before. We explained it is just creme anglaise. He still wasn't sure what it was, but the next morning he had apple pie and custard for breakfast, and he was hooked. We didn't see them again after that morning, but I'm sure he had lots more custard after that. It was nice to think that when he got home to France, he would sing the praises of English cuisine and our delicious custard to his French family and friends, and we were satisfied to know that we had promoted the spirit of Entente Cordiale while walking in the foothills of the Himalayas.

The temperature had dropped quite significantly overnight, and we woke to a keen frost. In most years this is not unusual for late October, but we had heard that the weather this year had been rather warmer than normal. Still, we weren't complaining, the sky was blue the air was clear and the view of Annapurna 2 was wonderful. But as good as the day felt, Deb did not feel the same. Her cold had become a lot worse. She hadn't got a fever but she felt quite poorly. If you knew her, you would know she must feel pretty bad if she says she feels ill. She is the type of person who would have to be at death's door before having time off work, and she hates taking medication or seeing a doctor. So when she said, "I don't feel so good," I knew she must be feeling very ill. She decided to start taking the antibiotics we had picked up in Pokhara. I suggested staying at Upper Pisang for a couple of days and resting up, but she wouldn't hear of it. She would rather get to Manang where we had planned to have a rest day. So on we went.

7

AT THE EDGES OF LIFE

We left Upper Pisang that morning knowing that from here, until we had crossed Thorong La, we would have to get used to the cold, and the thinner air. The landscape was very barren, rocky and above all, very dusty. The strong winds seemed to arrive at midday without fail, and then the dust was horrendous. It went everywhere; in your eyes, in your ears, up your nose everywhere. We even had to put our rain covers over our bags to stop the dust from getting in.

If we hoped to trek to Manang today, there was no time to lose. There was a very steep hill to get up, and with the thin air and Deb feeling ill, it was going to be challenging. However, the going at first was fairly flat and easy, which given Deb's condition was a blessing. We soon came to a very, long mani wall. This is a wall made of slabs of stones with prayers carved into it, and it was like none we had seen before; there were piles of very small stones stacked on wooden shelves. They looked like they had been there for a very, very long time.

Some of the Buddhist artefacts we came across were

amazing; the prayer wheels, chortens and mani walls have all been made with such care and devotion. In some ways, it made me envious that the people who made them had such strong faith. Don't get me wrong, I have faith in a supreme being, whether you call that being God, Allah or Brahman I'm not sure it matters, but I do believe we are all part of this Being's plan. I don't worship in a building, and I'm not affiliated with any organised religion, but there are times when I feel the presence of God, especially when I'm surrounded by nature. We have four children, and I was present at each of their births. I saw each one of them take their very first breath and witness their lives beginning. Some might say these are magic moments, but I would call them divine moments. New life was being created right in front of my eyes. These are incredibly special moments.

In 2015 I lost my dad. He had been struggling with Alzheimer's disease for about six years. Mum became too frail to cope with him at home and he had to go into care. The last eight months of his life were particularly difficult as he had a series of hospital admissions with pneumonia. He was frequently in and out of a coma. He was such a fighter though, and would not let go of life. On the night he died, we got a phone call from his care home. The nurse said she didn't think he had long to go. These nurses have vast experience in caring for people who are on an end-of-life care plan, so I knew she was probably right. I called round to pick up my Mum and my niece and we travelled down in silence to see my Dad. When we got there it was obvious that he didn't have long left. His breathing was like nothing I had witnessed before. His face looked so painful as he tried to suck air into his lungs. Then there was a very long period before his next breath. I held his hand and Mum held his other hand. I told him it was time to let go, he didn't have to fight anymore. I told him I loved him and that he had been a fantastic Dad. I told him not to worry I would look after Mum. He fought on for another ten minutes, he just wouldn't let go, he didn't want to leave Mum. Eventually, the time between the painful breaths became longer and longer until he took his final breath. Then his expression changed from pain to peace, and I felt a presence which I believed was divine. There's a song which we played at his funeral; *My Young Man* by Kate Rusby. In the song, there is a line: 'If someone's watching up above, you'll see how much my dear I love, and if he must go, let your best angels keep him well'. I believe there was a divine presence at the moment he died, maybe it was God, maybe it was his best angels, I'm not sure, but something special was there. Just as there was when each of our children was born. It's these moments at the edges of life, when life begins and when it ends, that we glimpse what is beyond. Somehow the veil between life and death becomes thinner and it is possible to get a sense of what is beyond.

I don't need a religion to tell me what to believe; I know what I believe. Some say God is everywhere, and I think I would agree with that, but it's easier to spot him at the edges of life and amongst the hills and mountains. And at that moment we were surrounded by the most wondrous mountains we have ever seen. I guess you could say we were in Paradise.

We crossed the river on another long suspension bridge and soon after started the long, tough climb up to Ghyaru at 3670 Metres. I think this was the toughest climb we had done so far. We could see the prayer flags of Ghyaru high above us, and it looked a long way off. The path went steeply upwards through many, many switchbacks. The thin air made it difficult to breathe and our progress was painfully slow. I'm not sure how long it took to reach the top but when we got there, we were knackered. Fortunately, we could get some black tea and a sit-down in the shade. We shared a Snicker and looked at the view back down the valley and the snow-capped mountains. We were here in Nepal, and we were trekking the Annapurna Circuit. Sometimes I had to pinch myself to make sure it wasn't just a dream, and I would wake up with my alarm beeping ready to go to school and teach my bottom-set year eleven the fundamentals of electricity. I didn't wake up. I was here. And, as they say, I was living the dream.

Ghyaru is an amazing village with houses built on top of each other. How many thousands of people had trodden its narrow walkways over hundreds and thousands of years? History and ancient things can make me feel very, very small and insignificant; like I'm just passing through, just another traveller in time and space. I love looking at old stuff; it gives me a perspective on time and allows me to put my own existence into context. So when I see an ancient stupa or a well-worn path and they're a few hundred years old, it enables me to imagine what they saw and maybe what they felt. When I look at rocks and fossils the time scale jumps to millions of years, but our Solar System is almost 5 billion years old, and it is made from a recycled star that exploded billions of years before our world and solar system existed; just as our entire bodies are made from the same stardust from a time when the universe was still young. However, the piece de resistance has got to be, that our bodies are made up of billions of atoms, and every single one of them was created in the Big Bang nearly 14 billion years ago. What was here before that? Your guess is as good as anybody's. Now that is something to try and get your head around. And, long after our bodies have returned to dust, the atoms of which we were made, will still be here, and going through the process of recycling again, and again, and again, until the end of time itself. In the words of the Eagle's song *Hotel California*, 'You can check out anytime you like, but you can never leave'.

The track to the next village of Ngawal was fantastic. There's a saying in Nepal that Nepalese flat is 'a little bit up and a little bit down,' and that's just how the trek to the next village felt, up and down, but nothing too steep, and never, ever flat. We came across a small tea shop on the side of the track. It was only open during the high trekking season, so we had a tea stop. I tried the coffee. Well, the guy said it was coffee, but I wasn't convinced. He was also selling chocolate cinnamon buns, so we gave them a try. They were as dry and dusty as the paths we were walking on, but we didn't complain as the young guy was very friendly and sociable. He pointed out the names of all the mountains we could see, and where Ngawal was. We wished him good luck and off we went. Ngawal is another old and beautiful village with amazing views, but we didn't linger as we wanted to get to Manang as soon as we could. The morning's efforts had drained Deb of energy and she was almost running on empty.

The rest of that walk felt like a battle. The wind had arrived and I was struggling, so God knows how Deb must have felt. The dust was horrendous and the sun was beating down. It started to feel like a scene from one of those old movies where some poor fools were trying to walk out of the desert in a sandstorm. To make matters worse it was one of only a few occasions when we weren't too sure of the way; not lost exactly, just a little disorientated. There seemed to be lots of paths forking off in all directions. Luckily a guided group came by and we asked if they were going to Manang.

A Walk Among Giants

They were, so we let them get a minute in front and then followed them. It is hard to put into words just how tough it was, but it was probably the hardest couple of hours walking through the entire trek. I could see that Deb was at the end of her tether, and that hurt, as there was nothing I could do to help. We just had to keep going, we couldn't stop here, and we had to get out of this dust storm. Finally, out of the swirling dust, a small village loomed up. It wasn't Manang, but by then we just didn't care. It was the village of Braka, which is about half an hour's walk from Manang. This would do. We weren't going any further today. We came to a lodge: The New Yak Hotel. Nepalese people have a great sense of humour. We went in. The sign said, 'hot shower'. Now we'd been here before, and seeing is believing, so I asked the rather strict-looking owner if I could see the shower. She looked a little annoyed but led us around the back of the building to where the 'hot' shower was located. She opened the door and we peered in. All appeared normal; concrete floor and bare, stone walls, so I asked her if I could feel if it was hot. Her expression was now looking very annoyed and the look she gave me told me I was pushing my luck to its limit, but she turned on the shower and it was hot. "We'll take a room," I said. I'm sure she thought me very rude, but we both desperately needed to wash the dust off, and because Deb was so unwell, it had to be a hot shower.

We quickly settled into our room and then shared a hot shower. I was more worried than ever about Deb, she was not only shattered but she was feverish and shaking. I got a couple of paracetamol down her and she laid on the bed. I covered her with her sleeping bag and she fell asleep. A long two hours went by. If my legs hadn't been so stiff and tired, I would have been pacing the floor. But, I was too tired so I just lay on the bed next to her. I had so many questions running through my head, but the number one question was 'What do I do if Deb gets worse?'

She didn't get worse, in fact when she woke up she felt a little better and wanted something to eat. Relief! It's such an underrated emotion; it always seems to take a back seat to the 'biggies', like love, happiness and anger, but relief really can hold its own in the emotional league tables. It brought me to tears I can tell you. It was good to see Deb eating a meal, and my worry, although it didn't disappear, faded into the background a little. I still didn't feel we were out of the woods just yet.

We both had a very fitful sleep and woke early. Deb wasn't up to walking today, but I managed to persuade her to have a little breakfast. After that, she went back to bed. I asked the lodge owner if we could stay another night then took up my position laying next to her. What else could I do? I didn't want to leave her and explore the village in case she woke up and needed something. Instead, I looked at the map and our itinerary and tried to work out a plan of how many days we could afford to rest up. My thoughts were: if we rested here for five days, we would still have time to complete the circuit, and if Deb still wasn't fit in five days, we could get a jeep back down the trail. However, if we did stay here for five days, we wouldn't have time to go to the Annapurna Base Camp as well. The Base Camp was an add-on extra that we were hoping to have time to do. It all depended on how long it would take to get Deb well again.

Deb slept for a good three hours, and when she woke up she felt pretty ropey. We had read in the guidebook that Manang had a medical centre. Now Manang is only half an hour's walk away, so Deb quickly got dressed and we set off to find it. It was an easy, level path to Manang but we still walked very slowly. There was a sign on the door of the Medical centre that said it didn't open until 1 pm, so we went into a cafe and had tea and biscuits then a little wander around the many tiny shops. At 1 pm we went back to the medical centre. The doctor was Canadian and a volunteer. He worked 6 months each year for the Himalayan Rescue Association. He gave Deb a good examination and his diagnosis was that she had a viral infection. He told her to stop taking the antibiotics as they wouldn't do any good and it should clear up on its own. He said if she started coughing more and producing more mucus, then go back on the antibiotics, but other than that, she just needed to rest. He checked her oxygen level and it was as good as the local population, so that was an encouraging sign.

We went back later to the medical centre, as they have a free lecture every afternoon on Altitude Mountain Sickness. It was an interesting lecture. We knew some of it as we had researched AMS and how to avoid it before our trek. But there were a few points we didn't know. For instance, older people are less likely to develop HACE, High Altitude Cerebral Edema, because as we age our brains shrink and this means we have more space between our brain and our cranium, so the pressure doesn't build up as quickly. Also, I believe that our bodies react to the lack of oxygen by producing more red blood cells. The doctor said that it would take about nine months at high altitudes before our bodies would react in this way. So the good news is because we're older we have less chance of getting HACE, but the bad news is our brains have shrunk.

Now my job was to get Deb to rest. If you knew her, you would know she doesn't do resting, so I have an impossible task ahead of me. It would be easier to herd cats than to get Deb to take things easy. Resting is not a word in her vocabulary; she is one of life's busy people, and she gets bored very easily.

We walked back to Braka and our lodge, and I told her about my plan to maybe hold up here and rest for five days. You can probably guess the reaction I got. She had other plans. One good thing to come out of it though was her determination to get herself better. She ate lots and drank lots of water. Where there's a will, there's a way, and she had the will to make herself well again.

We slept better that night and had a good breakfast. We planned to walk the half hour up the road back to Manang and book into one of the hotels. At least this way we were still making progress around the Circuit, even if it was only slight progress. Momentum is so important on a trek, and we had lost ours. We booked into a lodge and I put my foot down and told Deb "We are going to stay here until you are well".

She said those two little words that always could throw me off balance: "We'll see."

There's an old saying in Yorkshire 'You can always tell a Yorkshire man, but you can't tell him much'. Well, this must apply to Yorkshire women as well, it didn't matter what I said, she would decide when to move on.

We dropped our bags in our new lodge and Deb fancied a small walk around Manang. I agreed as long as it wasn't too far, after all, she was supposed to be resting. Manang is one of the largest villages on the Circuit, and there are lots of shops selling hiking gear and numerous cafes and places to eat. There is even a cinema showing films about mountains and mountaineering. For all these Westernised luxuries, it still had the look and feel of a town from a cowboy movie. I half expected Clint Eastwood to walk down the street ready for a gunfight. We ended up walking down to

Gangapurna Lake. It was an easy walk down and it was a very beautiful spot. We sat by the lake and looked up to the Gangapurna glacier high up on the mountain. We drank some water and ate coconut biscuits. I took a photo of Deb wearing my Tilley hat. She tried to smile but her nose and mouth were in such a poor state of repair that she couldn't manage it. Her lips and nose were red and angry and more than a little painful. The illness was taking its toll on her. It was a harder walk back to the hotel but we took it slowly.

The evening was spent eating, resting and looking through the guidebook. While we were waiting for our food to arrive, we saw what we thought was a mouse running behind some cupboards. A little later, while we were talking to another group of trekkers, we could hear what sounded like loud scratching sounds coming from a stack of sacks containing rice. One of the girls said that she had seen a rat earlier. O fuck! Please don't let it be rats. Yes, it was rats. I haven't got a phobia of rats, but they do give me the heebie-jeebies. I had an encounter with a rat when I was pretty young and it left me with a mild fear and dislike of them, but I think most people have similar feelings for these large rodents; they smell horrible, they cause damage and they carry and spread disease, what's to like about them? My first meeting with rats came when I was six years old. My best mate lived with his parents in an old, Victorian stone house. It was also the place of their fish and chip shop business. One day in the holidays we were playing hide and seek in the house, and I was looking for a place to hide. I opened a door thinking it was a cupboard. It was completely dark and I stepped in. It wasn't a cupboard. It was the steps leading to the cellar. I crashed down the steps and landed on the cellar floor. There, illuminated by the light from the street grate, was a big, ugly rat. The scariest thing was, it didn't run away. It just stood looking at me, while I cried for help. My mate's Mum rushed down and carried me back up the steps. She sat me on the table and cleaned me up while I sobbed. She put butter on the large bump that was growing on my forehead. I'm not sure why she put butter on, but it's what my Mum did whenever we bumped our heads, so it must be the thing to do. Since that day, I have had a dislike of rats. If that rat had run away, I think I might have felt differently.

They say you are never far away from a rat, and that's probably true. Here in Nepal, and in particular, in these predominantly wooden lodges, I am sure there are lots of rats, living and breeding in the framework of the buildings. After seeing the rat downstairs scurrying around, I was especially vigilant.

That night, as I lay in my sleeping bag, I heard scratching under the floorboards in our room. There was no way I could sleep knowing I could wake up to a rat sitting on my face, or climbing into the sleeping bag with me to keep warm, so I got up and put the light on. I scanned the entire room for gaps where the ratty bastards could get in. The only place where they could squeeze in was under the door. I needed something to block the gap. I knew it couldn't be anything soft like clothing as the rat could chew through it. So I wedged my trekking poles very firmly into the gap. There was no way even a big rat was going to push them out of the way. I'm sure most, if not all, the lodges we have stayed in had rats, but we didn't notice them, so it was all good. It's when you see and hear them that it becomes an issue. It's an out-of-sight, out-of-mind kind of thing. In some ways, you have to admire them. They are survivors. If the world is ever plunged into a nuclear winter, they say the only things alive will be the cockroaches. But I'll bet rats will also be there. They will probably eat the cockroaches to survive. Never underestimate a rat.

The next day Deb said she was feeling much better. I wanted to believe her, I did, but she's a poor liar, and we've been together a long time and I know her so well. I knew she was just going to push herself to the limit, but short of tying her down, there was nothing I could do to stop her. She planned to do a side trek to aid acclimatisation. The trek she had in mind was to Ice Lake. Now Ice Lake, at an altitude of 4,600 meters, is not a hike to take lightly. From Manang, at 3500 metres, to Ice Lake is a height gain of 1100 metres. In this thin air, it would be a killer. We had bumped into the Three Amigos in Manang yesterday and they told us they had tried to get up to Ice Lake and had not made it to the top. They were used to carrying much heavier packs than us, so trekking up to Ice Lake, without their big packs, must have felt like flying to them. Couple this with the fact that they're twenty years younger than us, and virus-free, and the chances of us getting up there seemed quite slim. I could have argued with Deb; I could have pleaded with her; I could have locked her in the room, but I knew none of these methods would work. No force on Earth could stop her from trying to get up that bloody hill to Ice Lake. We could have done an easier acclimatisation walk, but no, Deb had to do the hardest. So I tried to think it through and see the positives; if we did it, and got into trouble, there was medical help pretty close by in Manang; if we didn't do it and just trekked on up to the High Pass, and then got into trouble, that would be far more serious, and I didn't fancy a helicopter ride. So this side trek was probably the best of two evils. I saw it as a test. So, Ice Lake it was then.

First, we walked back to Braka and then started up the mountain. The tracks were narrow and very, very dusty. It was going to be a hot day so we had lots of water. It was good to have only a day pack on, I'm not sure we could have done it with our full pack. We passed a small tea shack on the way up, but we didn't stop we just wanted to get to the top. This was by far the hardest hike we had ever done; every step made our hearts pound and we just couldn't get enough air into our lungs. I couldn't believe Deb was doing this, I couldn't believe I was doing this; we must be plain crazy. We both had a thumping headache before we reached the top. This was a little worrying, but we wouldn't be staying up here long, and it is good to trek high and sleep low.

When we finally got to Ice Lake we didn't realise it would be so big, but I was slightly disappointed that Ice Lake wasn't frozen and wasn't deserving of the name Ice Lake. But, give it another month, and it will probably be frozen solid; Himalayan winters are ferocious. Sheltering behind a stone wall we had chapatis and hard-boiled eggs and admired the superb view of the Lake with a stupa and more stone cairns than you could shake a stick at. We didn't hang around too long we needed to get back down into thicker air and try and shake this headache off. We called at the tea shack on the way down and had a milk tea. We sat outside with our drinks and looked at the beautiful mountain across the valley, and I couldn't help but admire Deb. She never ceases to amaze me, she is so tough, made of pure Yorkshire grit. Sometimes it feels like walking with a member of the SAS. It's times like these, just staring at the side of her face, that I feel an upwelling of love for her. At that moment in time, I didn't want to be anywhere else in the world, just to be here in the Himalayas with my Deb, I was in heaven.

It was a long walk back to Manang and our hotel, but

our spirits were sky-high. The trek was back on track. Thorong La couldn't be much tougher than Ice Lake, or could it? We would find out in about four days. Back at the hotel, we were too tired to shower in cold water, so I took our clothes outside on the roof and shook the dust off them. As we were so hungry after such a hard day, there was only one thing we fancied eating and that was dhal bhat with a large second helping as well. It would have been great to have a beer with it, but we're saving that pleasure until we've crossed the pass. We started nodding off in the dining room, so off to bed. Tomorrow is another day.

8

ONWARDS AND UPWARDS

Today we aimed to get to Yak Kharka, at 4050 metres, that's a height gain of 500 metres. It was bound to be a tough day, because of the thin air, but it would be a short day. We should get there by lunchtime. Deb still felt unwell but it didn't seem to be getting worse and she was adamant that we should crack on up the trail. I think she felt guilty that she was ruining the trip, which was nonsense of course. We took vows nearly 40 years ago to look after each other 'In sickness and in health' and I've had my moments that have put her through the wringer with worry, so she didn't need to feel bad about anything.

In 2005 our world was turned upside down when I suffered a heart attack. It started on a Thursday evening. It had been a very stressful day at school, and my last lesson of the day was with my toughest class. It was one of those lessons where you wished the clock would move faster. Don't get me wrong, I'm not blaming this group for my heart attack. I had been having pains for about a fortnight before this, but I had put it down to indigestion. Yes, that old chestnut! If you're reading this, and have indigestion pains that last more than a couple of days, GO TO YOUR EMERGENCY DEPARTMENT NOW. I wish I had.

So on that Thursday evening, the pain got worse, and I was very worried. These pains were nothing like I had experienced before. When I look back I can't believe I didn't just ring for an ambulance. Like a fool, I kept it to myself. However, the next day was Friday, and I rang work to say I would be in late and went to see my GP. He also thought that it was just indigestion, and so I went back to work and tried to carry on as normal. It turned out the doctor was wrong. He should have been more cautious and sent me to the hospital to get checked out. Fortunately, his mistake didn't cost me my life. If you have chest pains, bypass your GP and go straight to the Emergency Department.

The day after was Saturday, and Deb and I went for a 10-mile hike in the Yorkshire Dales. I didn't say anything to Deb, but I struggled to get up the hills. When we got back to the car, I was exhausted and I had pain in my jaw and every one of my teeth ached. I told Deb how I was feeling, and she told me "We're going to the hospital now!" We set off for Leeds and I was driving pretty fast as I wanted to get there quickly. "I'm sure it's just a false alarm," I said. "They'll probably just check me out and then let me go home"

"Maybe it would be best if I drove," Deb said with a worried look on her face.

Of course, it would. What was I thinking?

The Emergency Department at Leeds General Infirmary were superb. I was dealt with quickly; they hooked me up to an ECG machine, did my blood pressure, took blood samples, and very importantly gave me a large dose of dispersible aspirin and a blood thinning injection. The doctor told me, "You have had a heart attack."

In sheer disbelief, I replied "No that can't be right. I'm only 48 and I'm as fit as a fiddle." I continued, "You must have made a mistake."

She put her hands on my shoulders, looked me in the eye and said very slowly and clearly "You have had a heart attack!"

I burst into tears. Even though I had feared this was what had happened, it still hit me like a ton of bricks.

I spent about a week in the hospital waiting to have a stent fitted. All the while, the staff said I cannot get out of bed, not even go to the toilet. I wasn't allowed to exert myself until the stent was fitted for fear I would move the blockage and cause more damage. I told them I had hiked over hill and dale with it and it hadn't killed me, I'm sure I could make it to the toilet without falling down dead. I disobeyed their orders and used the toilet. I didn't want to use a bedpan. I think they knew I was doing it but they turned a blind eye.

I'll never forget the day they gave me the stent. I was given a disclaimer form to sign which detailed the risks of the operation. The part that said, 'Can cause a further heart attack that could lead to death,' was the most worrying part. I asked the doctor to explain, and he just reiterated the warning on the form. He tried to reassure me, but at the same time, he had to lay out the risks involved. After all, they are prodding around in your heart, so there are bound to be risks involved. I signed the consent form, then I began to pray. I don't care whether or not you believe in God, when you are in that situation, you pray for help. I also thanked God, I said, "If this operation goes wrong and I die, thank you so much for giving me this life. Thank you for my lovely family; Deb and my lovely kids. Thank you for my loving parents. Just thank you for letting me be alive in your

A Walk Among Giants

wonderful world." I know it sounds crazy, but it was like making peace with God just in case it was lights out time and I didn't have the chance to tell Him.

I was laid on a bed and a tube was inserted in an artery in my groin. It was pushed up through this artery and my body to my heart. This was a weird feeling. It wasn't unpleasant, just strange. While this was happening I could see a screen and the doctor said it was live images of my heart beating away. A dye was released from the tube and I could see its progress around my heart on the screen. The doctor pointed out where the blockage was. After this, he slid the stent into place and inflated a tiny balloon to open the stent in its position. All went well. As soon as the stent was fitted it felt like I could breathe properly again. It was literally like a weight was taken off my chest. I was wheeled back to the ward to recover. Deb and my Mum and Dad were there. Deb could stay with me but after a brief meeting with my parents, they had to leave. I have only seen my Dad cry twice before, that was when his Mum died and when my brother John died. But he was crying when he left me that morning, and that is something I'll never forget. He wasn't one for showing his feelings, and I can't ever remember him saying he loved me, but seeing him so upset and emotional spoke volumes, and is a very treasured memory of mine.

The next day they allowed me to go home but not before I had a stress test on a treadmill, and I started running. I couldn't believe it. I was actually running. This filled me with hope. I WILL get better, and I WILL get back out in the hills. I WILL!

Some weeks later I went back to see the same GP and told him what had happened and pointed out that he had got it so wrong. He put his head in his hands, and with tears in his eyes, he apologised over and over again. I told him we are all only human and we all make mistakes so not to worry. All's well, that ends well. There was no point in being angry at him; his reaction was enough for me.

I would soon find myself back in the hospital. I had been home for about three weeks and Deb had returned to work. I was still getting pains in my chest and I didn't feel right. It came to a head one afternoon when I was convinced that I was going to die. I got down all the documents relating to my pensions and life insurance and made a financial plan for Deb. I was convinced I would die that very afternoon; these were my very last hours on Earth. I wrote my final goodbyes to Deb and told her I was sorry that there wasn't more in our financial pot. I told her "You are the love of my life and have been everything to me. I will love you forever." I hoped that she would find my dead body, and not our two girls when they get home from school.

Deb came home, and I wasn't dead, but she could see I was in a pretty poor state. She drove me down to Leeds Infirmary Emergency Department. They put me immediately into the resuscitation area as my heart rate was only 18 beats per minute, and they feared that my heart could stop at any time. The extremely slow heartbeat had caused my oxygen levels to drop dramatically and that's why I was so confused and wasn't thinking properly. I was given adrenalin and regained my sanity. They kept me in overnight and monitored my heart rate. It dropped dangerously low again while I slept. My Beta Blocker dose was halved and I felt much better.

I had about 4 months off work and set about getting my strength back. Deb was amazing; she encouraged me every step of the way and picked me up when I went through dark moments. And, there were plenty of them. She was there for me whenever I needed her and for that, I can never thank her enough.

I returned to work and tried to carry on where I left off. But things had changed and would never be the same again; I had been through a watershed moment in my life and there was no going back to how things had been before my illness. Working in school is a stressful occupation and teachers are their own worst enemies. They take on too much and push themselves too hard. I wasn't prepared to do that anymore. This didn't always go down well with my department manager, but there was no way I was going to drive myself into another heart attack. Having a close call like that, made me realise that our time here is short and I have to make the most of life because it could end in a heartbeat. Deb had been there for me every step of the way and I would be there for her every step of the way up to the high pass of Thorong La. I just think back to the hike up to Ice Lake. It was like a trial run for the harder bits to come, and she did it. Anyway, whatever will be, will be, and we were off on the trail spinning as many prayer wheels as we could. You can't beat a bit of divine intervention, and we needed all the help we could get.

The trail was very busy now, as lots of hikers miss out on what they believe is days of trekking on the dusty road, and take a jeep to Manang. Fools! They have missed some of the best parts of the Circuit, where there are less crowds and more beautiful tracks. We realised it would be busy like this now until we crossed the pass. I hoped the lodges weren't going to be full as I didn't fancy sleeping in a dining room. It's an age thing; the older I get the more comfort and privacy I need, and sleeping on the long seats in a dining room does not constitute comfort or privacy in my book.

After walking with only a light pack for the past few

days, our bags felt like they were stuffed with rocks. We took a break and watched the birds on the ground looking for God knows what to eat, as it was just rocks and dust. They looked a little bit like large partridges, and they were called Snowcocks. I hoped that they weren't an omen that it was going to snow. I don't think we could have handled any extra difficulty; well I couldn't, Deb could probably have carried me over the pass on her back. These birds seemed to be thriving on eating something in the dust. There were also lots of very large Himalayan Griffons, a type of vulture, flying high above us. I'm sure they were looking at me and thinking, 'His fat arse will make a tasty meal'. Well, they could keep their beaks off my fat arse, I'm very attached to it. They could eat the Snowcocks instead. Nature can be so cruel; imagine saying my arse is fat.

I don't like walking with lots of others. It's that thing where you don't like to overtake as it seems like you're showing off. Then if you want to stop for a break, they pass you. And then you feel they are mocking you for trying to go too fast. But, if you don't overtake, you feel you're not doing what you want to do and walk at your own pace, and that's no good either. Then there are the trekkers who relish overtaking you as if they are somehow stronger, fitter and more experienced in the hills than you are. They usually have bright red or orange pants on. If not brightly coloured pants, they have some items of clothing that are red, or orange. They need to be seen, or what's the point of them being here if you know what I mean? Where do people buy these trousers from? I've never seen them for sale in the shops I go into. I'm pretty sure GoOutdoors and Cotswolds don't sell such offensive items. Or maybe they do, but I've just not seen them. Maybe they have different sections for different walkers. A member of staff could act like a triage nurse and guide you to the appropriate section for your personality. A section for those who want to keep a low profile while trespassing. This could be full of camouflage gear and subdued colours like black, greys, greens or browns. And another section for normal well-balanced walkers. These could have nice colours like dark blues and checked shirts. Then a section for show-offs, they could call it the 'Knob-head Section' and it could be stuffed with reds, yellows, oranges and fluorescent colours of every hue. They would have to have designer labels of course, and I'm not talking about Rab, Berghaus or Mountain Equipment, it would be Armani, Gucci and stuff like that. Is 'colourist' a form of discrimination? Maybe it is. To paraphrase the late and great Martin Luther King: 'Men should be judged on the merit of their character and not by the colour of their skin.' But maybe he should have added on 'But the colour of his pants is fair game.' Okay, maybe I've crossed the line, or as Debbie would say to me "I've gone too far again!"

But red trousers on a man! If my two lads wore red trousers, I would have to sit them down and discuss with them the error of their ways, or maybe just disown them. Come to think of it, maybe I should disown them anyway for trying to kill me by booking tickets for Nepal. My two girls could wear red trousers. I think women can get away with it. Red trousers would suit Abby, and Grace would wear red trousers just to annoy me, she does that kind of thing.

I prefer to wear dark clothing that blends in. This is because, before the Right to Roam Act came in, giving open access to land, we liked to trespass on the grouse moors, walking off-path and finding our own routes. A yellow or orange jacket would have stood out a mile and had the gamekeepers running for their shotguns. Deb loved using the OS maps and planning routes off-path. I remember once being on the moors somewhere in Swaledale, North Yorkshire, and the mist was right down. We couldn't see a thing. Deb would set the compass; 'put red in the shed and follow Fred,' that's how she would do it. Then I would hold the compass in front and follow the needle while she would count her steps. She had 124 steps for 100 metres. That way she could tell the distance we had walked. She did it so well, that we walked for about two miles over the boggy moors zig-zagging to avoid obstacles, and still came out within a few metres of where she had planned. I told you, she could have been in the SAS.

We reached Yak Karka. It had only taken us about four hours but we were done in. The first lodge we went to had no rooms left. Oh shit! The next one also said they had no rooms. Oh, double shit! But, as we were leaving we bumped into a guide we had first met in Tal. He asked us if we were staying here and we told him, "There was no room at the inn."

He ran back inside telling us to, "Wait here."

Two minutes later he came back out with a key for a room. They do say it's not what you know, it's who you know. We thanked him and went to our room to unpack. The best rooms have hooks to hang things on. Some only have nails knocked into walls, but that's good enough. All our gear was in separate dry bags and they had straps that made them easy to hang up. It always made Deb giggle when she saw my colour-coordinated bags all lined up on the wall. It was my routine, and routines are important when you're trekking, it helps you to remember to do the important stuff like purifying the drinking water with a chlorine tablet or making sure the small stock of toilet paper is replenished. That was very important, believe me it really was.

We went to the dining area and found a conservatory-style room. It was just a glass lean-to really, but for all intended purposes it was a conservatory. We ordered veg phukpa soup, which was a noodle soup crammed with fresh veg and it was hot and delicious. The sun shone down on the mock conservatory and we lounged there in the warmth. Deb beat me at cards, once again, and we looked at and refined the plan I had made during Deb's sickness, though our thoughts were never far from Thorong La. We were over 4000 metres now and breathing when moving about was getting harder. How much harder would it be when we get to 5416 metres?

The sun went down and it became very cold in the glass house, so we went into the main dining room only to find it was chock-a-block full. We managed to squeeze onto the end of a table and wait for our meal to arrive. The wood burner was in the centre of the room and there was no way the heat from it could penetrate the numerous bodies between it and us. We ate our meal and ordered a very early breakfast for the next morning. Then we went back to our room and put our alarm on very early before anyone else got up. We wanted to get to a lodge at our next stop, Thorong Phedi, before the crowds got there. We didn't want to risk being without a room.

I had a weird sleep that night; I kept waking up startled and taking in giant breaths of air. It felt like I must have stopped breathing in my sleep, and my brain woke me up to remind me that air is vital for me to stay alive. It happened several times in the night and each time I woke, my heart would be pounding seriously fast. I read later that this is quite normal at high altitudes, but it does mean you can say goodbye to having a good night's sleep until you get down to thicker air. Altitude messes with your body, and we're only at around 4000 metres. How do the real mountaineers manage when they get up into the death zone at over 7000 metres? And what would it be like on top of Mount Everest at 8848 metres? It's hard enough down here; the Diamox makes your fingers tingle, and you pee like you've had 8 pints of Guinness on Saint Patrick's night, and to top it all off, you can't sleep because your body forgets to breathe. It's bloody freezing as well, and I feel like an eighty-year-old when I go to climb a single flight of steps, and I'm just not built to use squat toilets. My clothes reek of stale sweat and I stink like an old tramp. I've been wearing the same underpants for a week and wish I was at home drinking red wine in a hot bath, eating fish and chips and sleeping in my comfy warm bed. These were the kinds of things that went around my head when I couldn't get enough oxygen to breathe at 2 a.m. But, it would be all okay in the morning, I was just having a moment of doubt. The sun, and porridge with honey, usually made me feel positive again.

The top of Everest must be amazing though. What an achievement that must be. How do you come down from achieving something like that? I just wouldn't get out of bed. "I'm not going to work, I've climbed bloody Everest" I would say. "What, you want me to wash up? Sod off, I've climbed Everest you know." Or maybe "You cut the grass, I've climbed Everest." So maybe it's a good thing I never did climb Everest, I would be impossible to live with. Deb would probably say I already am.

It wasn't porridge for breakfast, we went for the fried eggs with curried fried potatoes. I never thought I would be able to eat anything curried for a breakfast dish, but being on an adventure does this to you; it broadens your horizons. Before you know it, I'll be wearing red trousers. Not on your bloody life.

9

A RAG DOLL AND A PILE OF POO

The next morning we were the first into the dining room and we thoroughly enjoyed our eggs. A flask of tea washed it all down. We paid up and wandered out into the cold morning. It was a beautiful, blue-bird day and the sun shone brightly on the snow-capped mountains around us. The ground was frozen and we had to be careful of the ice as we set off onwards and upwards. This would be another short day of walking, but as Thorong Phedi is at an elevation of 4450 metres, we would be gaining another 400 metres height. And, at this altitude carrying a heavy pack, it would be tough. The virus or bacterial infection, or whatever it is, that has given us so much worry hasn't got any better. But, on the positive side, it hasn't got any worse either, but we are still concerned about crossing the Pass with this infection hanging over Deb. We had never been this high before so it was hard to know how we would react, the next couple of days would be unknown territory, and we kept our fingers crossed that all would go well. It should be okay. We had done everything right so far; we had ascended slowly and taken rest days, we had kept as hydrated as we could and taken the Diamox. The fallback was always, if one of us feels like AMS has started, we will just turn around and go back down 500 metres or so.

We crossed a long suspension bridge over the valley. The river far below is little more than a stream now. There is something very satisfying about tracing a river to its source. The Marsyangdi River was a torrent back in Besisahar, but now it's little more than a trickle. I know it's not on the same scale as Dr Livingstone tracing the source of the River Nile, but for Deb and I, getting to the beginning of the Marsyangdi River felt like something special and worthy of a small celebration; so we broke out a Snicker and toasted our achievement.

We were coming up to the landslide area. This is an intimidating area of giant scree slopes. Looking up at the slopes we could see boulders perched precariously above. One little nudge and they would come crashing down on our heads. Our guidebook says many walkers have been injured here, and at least one trekker has been killed in the last few years. In recent times sections of stone retaining walls have been built to provide some shelter and protection from falling rocks; our mantra was 'If rocks start to fall, get behind a wall'. The landslide area takes about 15 minutes to cross and there was an ominous sign which warns trekkers to 'Step Gently'. Our trusty guidebook recommends trekkers walk ten metres apart and listen carefully for falling rocks. Well, the crowds had built up so we had a break before we crossed the danger zone and let several large groups go past. They can't have read the same guidebook as us because they didn't separate by ten metres, also they nearly all wore earphones so wouldn't hear falling rocks until they knocked their silly bloody heads off. I don't think they were stepping gently either. To top it off, I'm sure one or two had red trousers on, so there you go. Anyway, we let them go first. If there were any loose rocks, they would disturb them before we crossed. Then we went for it. No ten-metre separation for us though, as always we stuck together. If my Deb was going to be knocked off the mountain by a bloody rock fall, then I was damn well going to go with her. We scurried along, looking and listening for any signs of falling rocks, and we were relieved to get through it without incident.

Thorong Phedi was only a short way to go now, and we were ready for a cup of tea. As we got there we looked up at the path we would be going on in the morning up to High Camp. It looked pretty terrifying. It was a very, very, steep boulder slope. The trekkers already going up to High Camp looked like ants moving up the path high above. It sent my stomach into knots. I have a fear of heights. I've managed to keep it in check for years now. I push myself into scrambling situations where I can conquer my fears, but now and then it rears its ugly head and I go into a cold sweat. I think having a fear of heights, is a little like being an alcoholic. They say once an alcoholic, always an alcoholic. It's just the same with the fear of heights. You can conquer your fear for a while, but not permanently; you can win the odd battle, but the war still goes on. I would just have to deal with it tomorrow.

We booked into a lodge called The Thorong Base Camp Hotel. It was one of the largest lodges we had stayed in. Our room was in one of the outbuildings, and it had a toilet attached. This was always something I was glad to have; there is nothing pleasurable about having to get out of your warm sleeping bag in the middle of the night and get dressed to scuttle along to the communal toilets. We didn't ask if they had a shower, as it was far too cold to be fussing over small things like keeping clean. I think most people on the trek were pretty smelly by now, but it was something you didn't notice, as we were all in the same smelly boat together. We got comfortable in the large dining room. It was a very warm and congenial space. The guy who ran it was wearing a large cowboy hat and had the longest dreadlocks we have ever seen. We named him 'Supercool Guy', and he had a very expensive-looking stereo system on which he played our kind of music. There was Neil Young, Bob Dylan, The Eagles and of course Bob Marley. He played a great selection which helped pass the afternoon on. We played cards and put our journals up to date while eating cakes and apple pie and chatting to other trekkers. We met two young American couples. They had tried to reach High Camp earlier that morning but one of the girls had felt unwell, so they decided to come back down and try again tomorrow. They were nice people and easy to talk to.

We also met a very interesting Russian couple. I'd say she was our age but he was quite a bit younger. She was called Natasha and she spoke very good English with a great Russian accent. He was called Oleg and spoke no English at all. Natasha was very extroverted and confident and enjoyed introducing herself to everyone in the room. In contrast, Oleg was the complete opposite. He looked very uncomfortable and you could tell he felt out of place in this room full of people. Natasha told us her husband Oleg was very shy but very strong. I believed her; he was built like a brick shit house.

Everybody had plugged their phones and computers into the wall sockets to charge up. A cocky-looking American guy was looking around for an empty socket, but they were all being used. So he decided to unplug someone's phone and plug his computer in. He then plugged the phone into his computer so it would also charge up. What he didn't realise is, the phone he had unplugged belonged to the intense, Russian, brick, shit house. On seeing his phone being unplugged, Oleg moved effortlessly through the room. I say effortlessly because when people saw this very large guy with an expression that could kill at fifty paces, they moved out of his way, and silence fell in the room. When the American guy saw the Russian brick, shit house coming his way, he seemed to visibly shrink. He tried to explain what he had done, and that Oleg's phone would still charge up. He didn't reckon on the Russian not being able to speak English. The shrunken American, very sensibly, backed down and Oleg restored his charger into the socket. Back to his seat, he went, and Natasha turned to us with a broad smile on her face and reiterated the words "My husband is very strong," and no one in the room would dispute that. Yes, it was an interesting afternoon; good company and excellent entertainment.

That night we had a cold and disturbed sleep. We woke extremely early as people were moving noisily around getting ready to have an early start. They were probably going over the pass that day. We, on the other hand, had decided not to do that, we were going to have a night at High Camp. So by the time we got up for breakfast, most people had gone and we had our meal in peace.

I had decided the only way to tackle the steep boulder field was to do it one step at a time and keep looking down at the path. I tried not to look up at where we were heading or look down to where we had come from, just at where I was putting my feet. Deb knows what I'm like in these situations and she distracted me with conversations about anything and everything. I know why she does it, and I appreciate my mind being taken off the impending fall to my death. She looks after me well, my Deb. The path was incredibly steep, and it zig-zagged left and right, but always upwards. We had to negotiate around giant boulders the size of houses, and I imagined one coming loose and squashing us never to be seen again. In reality, it was extremely unlikely that the very large rocks would move, it was the smaller rocks falling from high above that posed the greatest danger. Perhaps we should have brought crash helmets with us. Before very long we made it up to High Camp, and we were still in one piece.

High Camp is one large lodge with lots of outbuildings, or chalets. Whatever you decide to call them, they were the usual small rooms; empty but for two single beds with a blanket and pillow. The main building had a large dining area with lots of windows offering fantastic views. We shared a flask of black tea and made a plan for the day. It had only taken 1 hour and 15 minutes to get here, and part of us thought it might have been a bit premature staying there, we could have maybe gotten over the pass today. However, I'm glad we decided to stay here. High Camp was a strange place, and I'm still not sure if I liked it or not. It was a cold and barren place and it was so difficult to keep warm. On the other hand, there were lots of short trails to wander on that gave great views and allowed ample opportunity to take fantastic photos.

After we had drunk our tea, we climbed up a hill behind the lodge that had a fantastic viewpoint. There were hundreds of cairns that people had built over God knows how many years and on top of the hill was a giant cairn covered in prayer flags blowing in the wind. The views from here were spectacular. We could see down to Thorong Phedi far below, and we had the place entirely to ourselves; everyone who had stayed here last night had already left to cross the Pass, and those who would walk here from Yak

Kharka wouldn't get here for a few hours. I think that's what made it such a magical place, it was the solitude away from the crowds, even if it was for only a short while. We even walked part of the way up the track we would walk tomorrow when we set off to the Pass.

Back at the lodge, we saw an event unfolding that emotionally affected us. A girl had been carried down from the Pass by a couple of porters. She looked in a bad way. She was unconscious and the only way I can describe her is that she was like a rag doll; she was all floppy and her arms and legs were flailing around. They brought her into the dining area and a Nepalese guide was speaking on a radio phone. We couldn't tell what he was saying, but we found out later that a helicopter had been requested. She was suffering from High Altitude Cerebral Edema, and it looked terrifying. We had to hold the tears back. She looked about the same age as our youngest daughter, early twenties, and we thought her parents would be at home now not knowing that their daughter was in such a perilous situation. They carried her back out and a little further up the hill where there was a helicopter pad. They waited there for what seemed like ages. Eventually, they brought her back inside. Someone said the helicopter had been diverted and they had to wait for another to be sent. This was a worry, as if she didn't get oxygen soon she could suffer permanent brain damage.

We couldn't watch any longer as it was too upsetting, so we went out for another short walk. On our way back to the lodge we heard the helicopter and saw it land. Thank God! We never did find out what became of her, but we hoped she was okay and it all ended well for her. The whole thing shook us up. High altitude kills people and you just can't take chances, you have to respect the mountains or they will bite you in the backside. You can't take shortcuts. The sight of that poor girl looking like a rag doll will stay with us for a very long time.

It was extremely cold. Eating was the only way to keep warm. We had dhal bhat, veg fried rice, cheesy omelettes, momos and cakes; anything hot with lots of calories. When we're at home, I get a bit of stick for eating too fast. But, here in the bitterly cold High Camp, that skill was in demand. You had to eat your food as fast as you could before it went cold. In the early evening, they lit the stove in the middle of the dining room and the place warmed a little, and I do mean a little, maybe a few degrees. There was no wood to burn as there are no trees, but there are a lot of yaks, and yaks poo a lot. They gather the poo up and squash it onto a south-facing wall to dry out. They look like beef patties but taste like shit. Not that I know that for certain, but it's a good bet. However, they burn well. The place had filled up and it had become very noisy, with everyone excited about going over Thorong La in the morning.

It was time for bed, although I wasn't sure we would get much sleep. We had seen a sign on the wall 'hot bags, 300 rupees'. We weren't sure what they were, but just the word 'hot' had us hooked. We got one each. It turned out that they were hot water bottles, just like the ones we had when we were kids. The smell of the hot rubber took us back to the days before central heating and double glazing, when in winter the insides of the bedroom windows would freeze and you could scratch out your name on them. I can still remember my Mum pouring hot water from the kettle into the hot water bottle and tightly screwing the top on. We had come full circle because that's just what it was like here.

We made a toilet break before we took our hot bags to bed. The toilet was outside and it was the most disgusting toilet we had ever been in. It wasn't too bad during the day, but now the temperature had plummeted, it had frozen solid. It was a porcelain squat toilet and it had been very well used over the last few hours. But it had not been flushed away down the hole, instead, there was a large mound of frozen shit. It was every colour of brown you can imagine with some green deposited for contrast. It was a pile of poo on steroids and not to be taken lightly, this poo could do you some serious damage. It looked almost malevolent like it might jump up and splat you. There was probably enough bacteria and DNA in there to make a new life form. But, I was desperate, and when you've got to go, you've got to go, and I had to GO. Trousers down, I tried to squat over the mound, which wasn't easy; it was like trying to get on a horse without letting your arse touch the saddle. I held my breath and tried to think nice thoughts, but they just kept coming back to the enormity of my predicament. Now, there was thick ice over the porcelain so getting a grip with your feet was more than a little tricky. If ever crampons were needed, it was now. There was no light either, so trying to see just using a head torch added to the drama. I should have filmed it really, Ridley Scot could have used it in one of his scary films. It would have fit into the Alien movie dead easy. There would have been film-goers in the cinema hiding behind their popcorn, shouting, "Tell me when it's gone!"

This is the kind of stuff guidebooks just don't cover. And, maybe they should, after all, it's all part of the trekking experience. Yes, one slip and I would have been covered in experience, with no hot water or facilities to clean it up. It could have turned into a disaster. I've been in the shit many times in my life, but it's usually hypothetical, never like this. After a couple of minutes of balancing, which a tightrope walker would be proud of, the deed was finally done, and I emerged triumphantly from the toilet. I turned to Deb and said: "Never mind giving it a minute, I don't think that would be enough, just don't go in!"

Well, Deb was also desperate so she didn't heed my warning, and with a deep breath, in she went. I waited outside hoping that I wouldn't be needed to pull her out of the medieval, mound of shit. I could hear several gagging sounds and I knew she must be struggling. I shouted through the door, "Breath through your mouth, not your nose." Finally, she emerged looking a bit green around the gills. We both agreed it would have been better to have gone behind the chalet for a 'wildy' and covered it with rocks. A horrible thought occurred to me: I hope they don't dry this shit out and burn it in the dining room. I know the Nepalese are resourceful people, but that would be taking recycling much too far.

As we suspected, sleeping was difficult. It was so cold and we both had headaches, and I kept waking up gasping for air, as I had forgotten to breathe again. We can't wait to get down to warm up at lower levels and breathe in good, thick oxygen-rich air. It will feel like breathing in warm custard or is that creme anglaise? Still, tomorrow would be a special day. The High Pass was waiting.

PART III

ENTERING MUSTANG

10

THE HIGH PASS

This was the big day. About 566 metres higher and there we would be, at Thorong La. Could we do it? Yes, we could, we were both feeling confident. We were well acclimatised and even Deb's sickness seemed to be getting better. We got up and dressed quickly, and I mean like our lives depended on it. It was like being in a deep freezer, even the water bottles in our room were frozen. Breakfast was eggs, toast and curried potatoes all eaten at record speeds before they got cold. I could eat cold toast and eggs, but not curried potatoes; they need eating while they're hot.

It was just getting light when we set off. It was about 6 am and the temperature outside was minus 15 degrees. But when the wind blew the wind chill factor made it feel much colder. Deb acted as a pacemaker as my body was still unsynchronised and I couldn't adapt my pace to the thin air. If I had set the pace, it would be stop, start, stop, start. That would not be a good idea. Deb kept a good pace; slow and steady. She kept checking if I was okay, making sure the dreaded AMS hadn't got me. She insisted on asking me what 6 times 7 is. "It's 42," I would reply. Every 15 minutes, the same question. What she didn't realise is that I had memorised the answer, so even if I had developed AMS, I would still be able to give the same answer, 42, although I would have probably slurred my words.

There were many ponies on the track here, and they were for hire. We saw lots of trekkers being transported to the top by horsepower, and not under their own steam. You can probably imagine the kind of language I was muttering under my breath when they went past. I mean why not just get a fucking wheelchair and get some big lads to push you around the whole bloody circuit. There's a saying: 'When the going gets tough, the tough get going' NOT, 'When the going gets tough the tough get on a bloody pony.' Deb could sense my displeasure and told me to "Stay calm, we're doing it the proper way and that's what counts". She was right. Deb can be very wise at times, and this was one of those times. This was not the time or the place to worry about other people's ethics, all we could do was do it our way. And that's just what we did to the very top.

There are several false summits near the top. Just as you think you're there and about to let out a 'Whoohoo', you see the path going further up. I'm sure it could be made into a method of torture. Eventually, we both could see the bright colours of the prayer flags which meant that we had reached Thorong La at 5416 metres above sea level. The highest point we had ever been. I thought emotion would have gripped me and I would be in floods of tears. I'm usually like that. I can cry at the drop of a hat if the occasion warrants it, and I thought this was going to be one of those occasions. Nothing! Not one single teardrop. I think I was too tired to cry, but my overriding emotion was euphoria. I was ecstatic to just be there. Sure there was a sense of relief as well, but nothing could detract from that feeling of bliss. The sun was shining and the sky was blue, and we could see for miles and miles. We held each other tightly and no words were needed. If I close my eyes now, I can still see the scene and feel the bliss of that moment in time.

There was only one way I could respond to this emotion, and that was to have a milk tea from the tea shack. Yes, at 5416 metres above sea level, you can get a cup of tea. So that was what we did, and of course, we had to have a celebratory Snicker as well, and then it was time for some photos. There was an informal queue waiting to get in front of the plaque to have their pictures taken. A large group of Spanish trekkers were waving the Spanish flag and singing their national anthem at the top of their voices. They were a loud and lively bunch, and most of them were wearing red, yellow and even orange trousers. But, under the circumstances, I thought it was appropriate to forgive them for their poor taste in hiking wear, as the colours were also the same as the Spanish flag, so good on them. And, how could I be critical of such a joyful band of colourful characters, when I felt like singing myself, and I would have gladly joined in with them if I had known the words to the Spanish national anthem.

We took lots of pictures of each other, and someone took photos of us both together. When I look at that picture now, of both of us holding hands in front of the plaque, I feel an overwhelming sense of pride. We stuck together and took care of each other, and there in that one photo, we stood side by side holding hands sharing and savouring that brief moment in time, when we could say, "We did it!" We both look thin and Deb still can't smile for fear her lips will crack open, but she was smiling the biggest smile ever, on the inside. We stayed at the top for about half an hour until the cold started to get to us, and then we started the very long trek down the other side of the Pass.

We were now entering the Mustang region. The descent was very steep and walking over small stones made it very slippery and treacherous in places. It was also a very long way down; the drop in height is about 1800 metres, so it was very important not to rush this bit, as every trekker will tell you prolonged descents are wearing on the knees. And, this was the longest descent we had ever done. It took about four hours to get down to Muktinath. Have you ever had one of those dreams where you're trying to get somewhere but you just can't reach it, and it just seems to get further away? That's just what this felt like. Our legs were aching. Our knees were aching. It was harder coming down from the Pass than climbing up to it.

There were some lodges near the bottom of the hill where we had something to eat and replenished our dwindling water reserves. The air felt great and it was much easier to breathe. The temperature was good too and we sat in the sunshine eating our meal of veg phukpa noodle soup and sea buckthorn juice. Now we were over the Pass, we could have a beer again, but not just yet, we still had over an hour to Muktinath.

Muktinath is a holy place of pilgrimage for both Hindus and Buddhists. It is surrounded by a large, white wall, and it is said that on this site all four of the natural elements are united: earth, air, fire and water. Well, there was lots of air around us and an abundance of earth in the form of rock. Yes, there is plenty of rock, everywhere you look. A stream runs through too. There is also a small fissure in the rocks here where natural gas leaks out. The gas is ignited and a small blue flame is displayed. The small blue flame is enclosed behind screens to make it easier to see. So all four of these natural elements are in one place, I'd say that's as good a reason for a pilgrimage as any other. It is good to know that people of different faiths can worship side by side. It's a positive step for peace in a world where conflict is commonplace, and there is religious intolerance. Pilgrims can bathe in two pools and walk under the 108 holy fountains. So you can worship, gain good karma, and get a good bath at the same time. They're clever these Buddhists and Hindus.

We walked passed the gate to the Muktinath temple complex, and shortly afterwards came to the village of Ranipauwa, where we would be staying. Walking under the archway to the village, we came to the first lodge The Path Of Dreams. This seemed appropriate as I was dreaming of a cold beer or two. We had heard that the quality of the lodges in the Mustang region was superior to the lodges in the Manang area. We booked in and we were not disappointed. We marvelled at the white, porcelain, western toilet. The toilet didn't flush so we had to use a bucket of water kept at the side to flush down. But we didn't care. After using squat toilets for the last couple of weeks, this was pure indulgence. The shower was hot, and so our first job was to get cleaned up. It was pure bliss, and we would have happily stayed under the hot stream much longer, but the second job was calling, to have a cold, celebratory beer. The hotel had a seating area on the roof, so we settled in there and passed the next hour enjoying a couple of well-deserved beers. The hotel also had Wifi, so we sent some photos and messages to the kids to let them know we had done the scary High Pass and were safe and sound.

We still had an hour to wait before our evening meal, so we went off to explore Ranipauwa. It had a long, wide street with lots of hotels and lodges. There were stalls selling silk scarves and jewellery. Others were selling religious paraphernalia. I suppose due to their location next to the pilgrimage site and on the Annapurna Circuit, business would be good. We came across the Bob Marley Hotel and we couldn't resist going in. It also had a roof terrace and we sat there and I had my first proper coffee for weeks. Deb doesn't like coffee so she went for a black tea. So we drank our beverages and watched the world go by on the fascinating street below while listening to 'No Woman No Cry' and still pinching ourselves that we made it over the pass.

The hotel filled up pretty quickly. We knew most of the other guests as we had met them on the trek over the last few days. The evening felt like a proper celebration. The atmosphere was great; everyone was having a drink or two and the place was filled with laughter and chatter. It also helped that the gas heater was left on to keep the place cosy. The heater was the same as the one in my Mum's kitchen and it looked a little out of place in the exotic dining room. I don't know whether it was the beer, the relief at getting over the pass, the thicker air, or just a combination of them all, but we slept like logs that night.

It was a good feeling getting up the next morning knowing that we would be going downhill for a change, and not slogging up steep inclines trying to breathe in the rarefied air. This was just as well, as our legs were very achy this morning, after yesterday's mammoth hike. We had a good breakfast and then set off up the main street to where the police checkpoint was. We checked in and then went back down the street. Most other trekkers were going in the opposite direction to us; they were carrying on walking the jeep road straight to Jomsom. We were taking one of the new NATT trails which went on the opposite side of the valley. But first things first, we paid another visit to the Bob Marley Hotel for a quick fix of coffee before the off. Deb also wanted to buy a small prayer wheel as a souvenir, so we stopped at one of the many stalls. It's expected that you will haggle over the price when buying anything, and Deb haggles like a local. I, on the other hand, am pretty rubbish at haggling. I either give in too easily or just give up and walk away; I'm just not that good at finding a compromise.

Mini prayer wheel bought and packed safely away, we found the start of our track. It headed down through a maze of small houses. The Mustang region has a very different feel to it. The buildings and chortens are painted with white, yellow and terracotta vertical stripes. We couldn't find out why this was, but maybe it was because we were so close to the holy site, or more likely it's just a cultural thing. The terrain had very little in the way of greenery and was mostly rocky, barren ground. However, around each village, the ground had been irrigated and cultivated to grow a variety of crops and we even saw many old, large trees. Perhaps they had been planted many years ago to provide shade in the long hot summers. It is often said that planting a tree is not done for oneself but for future generations.

The views over the valley were extensive, and we could see the dusty jeep road, which made us glad we had chosen this less-used trail. Our destination for today was Kagbeni. This was day 14 of our trek and we have become very comfortable carrying our packs. They don't feel as heavy as they did back at the start of the trek, and we have become fitter and stronger, and we've lost weight, which in my case was a good thing. Who needs to go to the gym, just get a pack on and do some trekking? The sun was shining and we both felt it was going to be a good day.

Although we were only just over halfway around the Circuit, we both felt relaxed, and happy to take our time, almost as if we were on the home straight. We weren't of course as we still had many more miles to go. We walked through the Tibetan-style villages of Chongur and Jhong. At Jhong there is an old ruined fort and a Gompa with a tea house close by. We explored the area and visited the Gompa. It is here we met a young couple who were to become good friends. Their names are Kieran and Helena. We all went to the Gompa together, and an old monk unlocked the door for us to have a look around. Inside it was dark and felt very ancient. Some very old musical instruments fascinated me, and I would have loved to have banged on the drum and gong, but I don't think it's the done thing. After we had finished our visit, we all went to the tea house for a drink and some soup. Kieran and Helena came over the pass, as we had done, the day before, but they had decided to have an extra day exploring the area around Muktinath, and generally taking things easy. We would get to know them both well over the next week, but for now, we went our separate ways.

We said our farewells and pushed on for Kagbeni. After a short while we came across a young woman selling apples, so we bought a couple for our journey. She also had some bracelets for sale, and as I had previously mentioned, I am a sucker for bracelets. I saw one I liked and started the usual, and expected, haggling process. Deadlock was soon reached; she wanted 400 rupees, which is about £2.80 and I wanted to pay 350 rupees, which is about £2.46. We haggled back and forth but she wasn't going to budge. Then I had one of those moments, we all get in life when things become clear and in focus. Almost, but not quite, an out-of-body experience, where we see the big picture and the things that matter, I thought to myself; why am I haggling over an amount that is about 34 pence? I am a relatively rich westerner and 34 pence is loose change to me. However, 34 pence means something to this woman. She has at least three children we can see, and she needs enough money to see her through the low tourist season. I gave her the 400 rupees she asked for and bought another bracelet. But, this time I didn't haggle like a greedy westerner. However, I still haggled a little, the Nepalese are poor but they are also proud people, and they don't want charity or pity. Lesson learned; we are all human beings and as such we are all equal. But equality doesn't stretch to economics. There are the haves and the have-nots in this world, and if you are in a position to help someone who has very little, it would be a shameful thing not to do so. Perhaps opportunities such as this one, are purposely put in our path. Oh heck, I think I am becoming a Buddhist.

Sporting my newly acquired bracelets, we carried on down the valley. It was beautiful with shades of autumn colouring the landscape. I wrote in my journal that evening that this had been the best day on the trek so far. It seemed like we were the only trekkers taking this route. Apart from Kieran and Helena, we didn't see any other trekkers at all. It made the day very special.

We soon came to a suspension bridge that would take us over a deep gorge. The terrain on the other side was very different. It was more like a desert; just sand, rocks and open space for mile upon mile. We followed a sandy trail that appeared to have tyre tracks on it. This was a very barren country of a type we had not walked on before, but that's one of the best things about the Annapurna Circuit; if you follow the new NATT trails, and do the whole circuit, the variety and diversity of the terrain is vast.

Scary moment number two was about to happen. A jeep with two men inside came up behind and went past us. We waved and they waved back. About five minutes down the track, we saw the jeep parked up at the side of the track. The two men had got out and were sat on a rock. Once again stress levels began to rise and the adrenaline started to flow. Bear in mind we were in the back of beyond and there wasn't a living soul anywhere for miles. We had no choice but to carry on and hope this wasn't going to end badly. This would be a perfect place to rob and murder a pair of hikers. It would be so easy to dig shallow graves for their bodies, and they would never be found out here in the middle of nowhere. We got closer and closer to the pair of men. One of them was talking on the phone to someone. We waved and just walked past. Crisis averted, or more accurately just a false alarm. I felt a bit silly for being so worried, but I think it's just a primal and biological reaction to a situation that could be dangerous. A little later we looked back and the jeep had turned around and was going away from us.

The walking was easier now, on a slight downhill incline. Soon we came to the top of an escarpment with a view to Kagbeni below. There appeared to be only one way down; the path wound its way through a large cleft in the cliff. The wind here was ferocious, and we had to shout at each other to be heard as it was so loud. It blew my glasses off my head, and we spent 5 minutes looking for them. We very carefully climbed down through the cleft. It wasn't a difficult climb down, but the wind threatened to knock us off balance or dislodge the many loose-looking rocks above our heads. It was a relief to get down and away from the cliff. Kagbeni was then only a short five-minute walk away.

We entered its narrow alleyways and began to navigate into the centre of the village. This place was amazing. It looks and feels ancient, like something from the Middle Ages. There was a statue on the side of one of the alleys. It was of a giant man about three metres tall with a large round head and a fierce expression, and he was wielding a sword. However, the most striking thing about him was his enormous, erect penis and a large pair of testicles hanging below it. Someone had hung some beads on it. He is known as the 'Protector of Kagbeni', but for obvious reasons, he had been named 'Mr Viagra'. The guidebook said he was there to ward off any evil spirits that might come into the village. I suppose evil spirits would think, if the men here look like this, we won't stand a chance, we better skedaddle before he sees us. Later we would come across 'Mrs Viagra', the protector's counterpart, who also had her 'bits' on display; however, her role was to represent fertility. Just off the main square, was a hotel that, once again, confirmed the Nepalese sense of humour, it was called Yak Donalds, and in place of the golden arches was a stylised image of the front view of a yak, in gold of course.

We booked into the Asia Trekkers Lodge. It was starting to get dark, and we were also pretty tired, so we decided to leave exploring this fascinating village until tomorrow morning. The lodge was pretty good, even the shower was hot. I thought I would have something a little different for our meal, and I went for a yak burger. It was delicious, but I didn't feel safe eating the salad that came with it. If it had been washed in untreated water, I could end up with a case of the runs. I wasn't going to risk it. The place was nearly empty, there were just us two and two elderly German women. It seems not as many trekkers visit Kagbeni these days. Most seem to go down the jeep road from Ranipauwa directly to Jomsom, where they fly back to Pokhara or Kathmandu. So it's getting harder for the lodge owners to make a living. This is a shame, as Kagbeni is a place not to miss. It has got to be one of the most fascinating villages on the whole Circuit.

11

THE THREE WITCHES OF CHHAIRO

We were up early the next morning as we wanted to have a good look around Kagbeni before we set off on the day's trek. There were lots of photo opportunities to take advantage of, and we were intent on doing some serious snapping. In a small courtyard, we stopped to take some photos of the amazing buildings, when an old lady came out of what looked like a tiny door of an animal shelter. She was the smallest adult we have ever seen; a perfectly formed person in complete miniature. She was dressed in the familiar traditional Nepalese garments and her face was full of wrinkles; she had the most striking smile that lit up her face. She looked about 100 years old, but her expression was full of life. Deb is 5 foot 2 inches and this lady was at least a foot smaller. We asked her if we could take her photo and she indicated it would be okay. Deb stood next to her and she towered above her tiny frame. We asked her how old she was, but she didn't understand us. We gave her 200 rupees and said goodbye. We both suspected that she probably did her 'wander' through the courtyard every time she saw tourists taking photos. But that was okay, there is no social security in Nepal, and she can't just pop down to the Post Office to pick up her pension. She has to rely on her family to provide for her, and if the occasional tourist happens to give her a few rupees for a photo, then good for her.

Continuing our walk around the countless alleyways and small yards, we dodged cattle and goats that seemed to just wander freely around the place. Then to our surprise, we came across an Applebee's coffee shop. We could hardly believe our eyes. Of course, we went in and had coffee and cake, well Deb had tea. It was wonderful inside, it wouldn't have looked out of place in the centre of Leeds. Nepal never ceases to amaze us; from a medieval ally through a door into a sophisticated, twenty-first-century coffee shop, all without a time machine. Amazing! I'm not sure how many photos we took but it was a lot. However, it was time to get trekking to our next stop which would be the large town of Jomsom. Though, we were quite sad to leave Kagbeni, in hindsight, it would have been a good idea to spend more time exploring and stay another night. Ah well, we were on our way now.

Kagbeni lies at the confluence of two rivers: the Chong River, which we had followed from Muktinath and runs through the middle of Kagbeni; and the bigger Kali Gandaki River, which we would be following for almost the rest of our trek. There are two routes to Jomsom; the road route, which will take about 2.5 hours; or the high route which our guidebook says is arduous and could take up to 8 hours. Of course, we took the high route, the thought of trekking on the dusty road for 2.5 hours was just unthinkable, especially as we had been told that strong winds blow up the valley every day starting at 10 am, and they get stronger by the afternoon. The dust on the road would have been unbearable. This was the same wind that blew my glasses off, as we had battled to get down the cliff yesterday.

We walked along the flat valley bottom, which was littered with millions of smooth, rounded rocks. We tried cracking some of these rocks open to find fossils inside; however, lady luck wasn't smiling on our fossil hunt, which is probably a good thing, we would doubtless have carried them with us. Fossils are made of rocks, and you would be crazy to carry rocks in your pack, wouldn't you?

There was a very small settlement up ahead which was called Eklebhatti, which sounds very much like it should belong in Yorkshire, a cross between Eke Thump and Nora Batty. Here we crossed the Kali Gandaki River on the longest suspension bridge of the trip. It's amazing the kind of traffic that goes across these bridges. Obviously, people are walking over on foot, but there are also mule and yak trains carrying enormous packs and gas cylinders, and sometimes, as now, it is a convoy of motorbikes. After the bikes had left the bridge, we crossed to the other side and started walking up, up, up. We wandered through the lovely village of Pakling and onto Phalyak. There is a lot of agriculture here, but lots of the fields had been harvested of their crops so the ground was bare. Most of the fields are enclosed behind very high walls to protect them from the strong winds and prevent the soil from being blown away. We watched a family working in the fields. The father was driving a pair of oxen, which pulled an ancient plough, while his wife and children followed behind him planting, what looked like seeds. Everyone was involved in this scene which probably hasn't changed for a thousand years. Everything here is designed to keep out the wind. Most of the villages have alleyways which are enclosed to make tunnels, like human-sized rabbit warrens. I wonder if the people here just get used to the wind and dust. I suspect they do. We have been lucky to have spent time on the Outer Hebrides, and there the people have adapted to the wet and windy conditions, it's just soft city folk like us that struggle with, what we think are, extreme conditions.

Shortly after Phalyak, we came to the lovely village of Dhakarjhong which had a large pond at its centre. The pond has been formed by damming a stream with a thick wall. Unusually, in the middle of the pond was an old chorten. On the wall was a plaque that said the work had been paid for by the Nepalese Ghurkas, and we sat there on the wall and had our packed lunch and some essential water. The weather was very hot now and walking in the full sunshine was hard work. It was probably fortunate that it was so windy as I'm sure we stank to high heaven. While resting there in the shade, a herd of cattle came down to drink. They didn't mind us being there, and we were happy to share the shady spot with them. This had a real feeling of what trekking should be all about. There was just us two on the trail, and the villages were a genuine insight into the real lives of the people of rural Nepal. It was Wonderful!

Leaving the village we could easily see our path, as we had to head for a telecommunications mast which was in clear sight on the top of the ridge. With our sunglasses firmly on and hats and buffs fitted tightly, we pushed onto the ridge. When we got there the wind was so strong it was difficult to stand up, especially Deb, she is so light it might have been an idea to anchor her down with rocks. Maybe it's a pity we didn't find any fossils. This high spot is called 'Batase Bhanjyang' which translates as 'Windy Pass'. The views from this point were fantastic though, and we spent a good 10 minutes taking photos. There were views back to Thorong La and superb views of Tilicho Peak, Nilgiri,

Dhaulagiri and Tukuche Peak. Deb's much better at naming the peaks than I am, and I constantly ask her which mountain is which. She gets mesmerised by the mountains and would spend hours photographing them if we had time. I have to confess, that I have, on the odd occasion, been guilty of being a little grumpy and impatient about Deb constantly stopping to take yet another bloody picture of sodding Dhaulagiri. "How many pictures do you need of snow-capped mountains?" I complained "Each picture is going to look the same, you'll end up deleting most of them. Let's just get to Jomsom and get out of this bloody wind and dust!" As you can see, I was pretty vocal about the things that annoyed me; the tireless wind and the omnipresent dust had robbed me of any patience I possessed.

Once over the ridge we still had a couple of hours to go and the trail wasn't easy; the narrow path was incredibly dusty and the wind whipped it up. Deb made me walk 100 metres in front so she wasn't walking in the wake of the dust storm I was creating, or was it because she was fed up with me constantly moaning? You would have to ask her that, but I think you already know the answer. Way down on the flat valley floor, we could see the river. There was a place where jeeps forded here, and we saw some jeeps parking in the water while the driver got out with a large brush and washed it down. If we were closer I would have gladly gone in the river with all my clothes on just to get rid of this dust. On a more positive note, if we had trekked in the rainy season all this dust would have been mud, and I think that would have been even worse. We would soon get to Jomsom.

On the outskirts of the town, we could see the runway for the airport so we knew it wouldn't be much farther. The last part of the trail involved a very steep and airy descent before hitting the jeep road. It had been a long, tough day, but we were pleased we had walked the more difficult high route. Again, we had hiked the whole day without any other trekkers in sight, and we had visited some amazing places. The tunnelled villages were unique and wonderful and we were so glad we had taken the time to see them.

We were at an altitude of 2720 metres, which is only 80 metres lower than Kagbeni, but the 'windy pass' had an elevation of 3435 metres so we had earned a beer tonight. As usual, we didn't know where we were going to stay, so we wandered into the town. This was not as easy as usual, as Jomsom is a very large and busy place. We ended up near a military barracks close to the airport and booked into the Xanadu Lodge. Once again we were pleased with the quality of the accommodation in Mustang. Our room had a large, comfortable double bed and an en-suite bathroom with a hot shower, but the most noticeable thing was it had a carpet. This was a first on our trek. The bathroom was of the wet-room style. I had the first shower and I noticed that you had to be careful the shower did not spray the door. If it did, the water ran down the door where there was no barrier to it escaping the bathroom. I told this to Deb before her shower, but I think she was so pleased to be showering the day's dust and grime off, that she either forgot or didn't realise what the consequences could be.

There was an urgent, almost frantic, knocking at the door. On opening it I saw a young Nepalese woman and she was pleading with me to turn the shower off. She said there was water dripping into the dining room and onto the food of the people eating their meals. I could see that soapy water was flooding under the door and had soaked the carpet, so I quickly told Deb to turn the shower off. From there the suds had gone through our floor and dripped into someone's dhal bhat. Deb was beside herself, "I won't be able to show my face downstairs," she said with a look of horror on her soapy face.

I told her "It wasn't your fault. It is a design fault in the bathroom. It must happen all the time. They need to fix it". I continued to reassure her, "The people downstairs won't know it was you who was responsible for ruining their dhal bhat. We'll just put a smile on our faces and brazen it out"

I managed to persuade her to come down and have a drink and some food. We chatted to a young Russian couple whose names were Victoria and Slava, and showed them a card game we play called 'Crash'. We should have realised the type of characters these two were when they asked a waitress if she would cook them some food they had brought in from outside and asked for a glass for bottled drinks they had bought in the town. Either they didn't understand the concept of a restaurant or they were just being plain rude. I believe it was the latter. The lodge owner came in with a face like thunder. I'm not sure what language she used but it was pretty clear by her tone and her body language that she was ready to evict them. The pair wound their necks in, put their food back in their bags and ordered a beer. The situation diffused and things settled down, so we carried on playing cards until an Indian couple asked if it would be okay to sit at the table next to ours. Deb told them "Of course it's okay. Please sit down."

However, Slava stood up sharply and said, "There's no room here, you'll have to sit somewhere else." He pointed to a table on the other side of the room, and said, "There is a much more room over there."

The Indian couple looked surprised and moved away from us and sat down on the opposite side of the dining room. We couldn't believe it. We were shocked. It was a blatantly racist thing to do. What made this Russian guy think he was somehow better than anyone else? What made him think he could treat people so badly? This world would be a much better place to live in if we all saw beyond a person's skin colour and looked for the real person inside. Our only regret is that we didn't say anything. If we could have turned back time, we would have handled the situation differently. That's the trouble with time though, it's a one-way street. I later reminded myself of the saying: 'For evil to succeed it is only necessary for good people to do nothing'. In effect, we did nothing, and that was something we both felt ashamed of. Looking back, I wish we had apologised to the Indian pair and asked if we could join them, but we didn't. An opportunity to do good had been missed. Let's hope we will be ready for the next time. We finished our drinks, made our excuses, and went to bed for an early night. It's so much easier trekking on the trail than having to navigate around human sensibilities and personalities. Give me the mountains any day.

We slept well; the bed was so comfortable and the breathing issues I had at higher altitudes had disappeared. Also, we had stopped taking the Diamox when we got over the Pass, and except for the antibiotics that Deb was still taking, we were drug-free. Maybe that has helped us to sleep better.

We had a good breakfast and walked out to meet the day. The village was bustling with people going about their business and we saw several light aircraft taking off. After the last fortnight of peace and quiet, this hubbub was quite overwhelming and we would be glad to leave Jomsom behind. There was a clean water station near at hand so we went to fill out water bottles. They use UV filters to kill any bugs or bacteria. These stations have been set up at various points along the circuit. The aim is to stop trekkers from buying bottled water, as it's difficult to get rid of plastic waste. We have noticed that lots of villages have small rubbish dumps on their outskirts which they periodically set fire to, so eliminating as much plastic waste as possible is a positive thing to do. The water is cheaper than buying bottled water so it's a win-win situation. Although to be honest, we still put a chlorine tablet in the water just to be on the safe side

Today we were heading for Tukuche, but we have a few other places of interest to pass through before we get there. Our first visit was to a typical Thakali village called Thini. We love these tiny villages; they are untouched by time, and it feels like a real insight into the lives of people from a bygone era. I suppose you could say we're like time travellers, or perhaps travellers in time and space.

The high mountain of Dhaulagiri dominated the view in front. It stands at 8167 metres and is the seventh-highest mountain in the world. It has that stereotypical pyramid shape. From the village, we climbed up a steep hill to explore an old ruined fort. It was a logical place to build a fort, as it was the kind of location that would have been difficult to attack and easy to defend. We had a break here and broke open another pack of coconut biscuits. Deb has a lovely ritual that she has been doing for as long as I can remember; she always throws some food down for 'the little creatures'. It could be part of a biscuit, like now, or part of a sandwich, whatever it is, she gives it to 'the little creatures'. And I think that is wonderful. We both have habits and idiosyncrasies that can be annoying, but we also have some that are endearing and quite lovely, and this is one of my Deb's.

Leaving the fort, we headed up a dirt road and soon came to a fenced-off area with a lake. It was Lake Dhumba. There were a few motorbikes there and some local teenagers enjoying a picnic. We had to pay a few rupees to gain entrance, but it was such a lovely spot we didn't mind. We took some photos and Deb did her best 'model' pose by the emerald green water and then we pushed on to get a few more miles under our belts. Today's trek to Tukuche is quite long so we had to keep an eye on the time. We climbed to a ridge and then crossed a very wide area of scree full of boulders. It looked like the rocks had been washed down during heavy floods. The stream, which is a tributary of the Kali Gandaki, flowed down the middle but it was quiet today, I'm sure after heavy rain or snow melt it would become a raging torrent. We crossed over to the other side and joined a fantastic alpine-style track which traversed the mountainside, undulating up and down as we went along. On the other side of the river, we could see the large village of Martha. We decided this would be a good place to have lunch. But first, we had to get to the small village of Chhairo on this side of the river, where there is a bridge we could cross to get to the other side.

Eventually, we came to the village. It was a settlement with a very interesting history. The People's Republic of China invaded Tibet in the early 1950s, or as they called it 'The liberation of Tibet'. It was a complicated and drawn-out process of annexation. The Chinese say they were liberating the Tibetans. The Tibetans say the Chinese were invading and taking control of their country. Well, you can wrap it up however you like, but when a large and powerful country, like China, which has a massive military force, walks into a small country like Tibet, which has an incredibly small army, I call that aggression and bullying on a giant, international scale. I'm reminded of the saying: 'Power corrupts and absolute power, corrupts absolutely'. The powerful Mao Tse

Tung, or Chairman Mao, developed his unique brand of communism, and nothing could stand in his way. Tiny Tibet was trampled on, but in 1959 an uprising began which inevitably failed and was crushed by the Chinese. The Dhali Lama fled to India in exile, and many Tibetans fled to Nepal. In 1960 the Red Cross Society was involved in trying to help the Tibetan refugees and they purchased the area of land we are now in; they helped them to build a village and form a community, which they named Chhairo. That's what makes this village special. Many of the refugees worked on new road construction and the new Jomsom Airport. The families living here now are direct descendants of those refugees who fled their homeland of Tibet all those years ago.

We crossed the road bridge and walked back up the road for about 20 minutes to reach Marpha. But on the road at the other side of the bridge, we got waylaid by 'three witches', well that's the name we gave them later. Each had laid out a sheet on the ground and covered them in trinkets of every description. Of course, I was immediately attracted to the bracelets. As soon as we showed any interest, they pounced on us. We didn't want to be rude to them, but we felt like telling them to back off and let us look in peace; a bit like used car salesmen, as soon as you open a car door, they're there trying to sell you the damn thing. I kept my cool and browsed like a professional. I saw a bracelet I liked and asked how much.

She said it was "800 rupees."

I laughed and said, "That's too much."

She said, "How much will I pay?"

I thought for a while, trying to appear as if I wasn't sure I wanted the bracelet. I thought it best to play it cool. "400 rupees," I replied.

She came back very quickly with a counteroffer of, "600 rupees."

I said, "It's a deal." I had learnt my lesson from my last haggling episode. She was happy with the price and so was I, or as a Vietnamese trader once told me 'Luck for you, luck for me'. Now the other two witches were all fired up; they had seen the colour of my money and I don't think they would have let me go on my way until I had bought some of their stock. Yes, you guessed it, I bought another bracelet and a pendant. Debbie took a picture of me with the smiling 'Witches of Chhairo'.

With my pack a little heavier and my wallet a little lighter we headed up the road to Marpha for some lunch. Marpha is in the heart of the Mustang apple-growing area, and we both thought it was the tidiest village we had been through. Its narrow streets were swept clean and some of the buildings were old with intricately carved wooden shutters. We found a lodge and ordered veg noodle soup and a glass of local cider. We had to try the cider as it was brewed locally and we were thirsty, and cider is always a refreshing drink on a hot day. We were surprised when the soup came so quickly, it usually takes at least half an hour.

We had a good rest in the shade and walked back down the road to the bridge. Even though our goal of Tukuche was on this side of the river, we wanted to cross back over to the trail on the other side rather than walk on the dusty road. Approaching the bridge we could see the three witches were casting their spell on some other unsuspecting trekkers so we managed to slip by unnoticed. Once over the bridge we turned right and began to follow the river.

I had a very uncomfortable feeling deep down in my stomach. Something wasn't right. I needed to find a toilet. On the outskirts of this tiny village, that was going to be impossible, so I looked around for a bush with suitable cover. The problem was that there were lots of children about and it didn't feel like the right thing to do just there. So we walked very quickly, or should I say I minced very quickly, a little further down the path to where the village ended and the cover was thicker. I dashed into the bushes with Deb's laughter ringing in my ears. "Oh, fuck!" I was too late. I managed to get my trousers down before the second wave came. I couldn't believe I could create such a smell. It felt like my insides had been through a blender and were now spewing out of my arse. I've heard of projectile vomiting before but not projectile shitting. During a pause in the proceedings, I looked backwards at the brown, expanding, puddle that was draining into the clumps of grass. Thank God I had a new toilet roll in my bag. I cleaned myself up the best I could, and walked back out of the bushes to my kind and caring wife laughing her bloody head off at me. But, not for long. Her expression turned from laughter, to surprise, and then to shock. She also ran into the bushes and had the same experience as I had just had. Now that was a serious case of instant Karma if ever there was one. Needless to say, when she emerged from the bushes I couldn't resist saying, "That'll teach you."

The rest of the journey to Tukuche went by in a blur, with both of us frequently dashing into the bushes and then returning with ashen faces. We blamed it on the cider, but I thought the soup was served too quickly. It wasn't freshly made, it could have been sitting in a warm pan breeding bacteria for hours. We will never know, but our son Tom always says, "You've not been on a proper adventure 'till you've shit yourself at least once." Well, I think that qualifies our trek as a 'proper adventure' then.

We crossed the river on a suspension bridge and walked

up the road for about half an hour before arriving in Tukuche. There was a higher path we could have taken, but it was getting late and the sun had gone down, and we were feeling very drained, literally. We went into the first lodge we came to. It was called the High Plains Inn. The lodge was run by a Dutchman and his Nepalese wife. He showed us to our room which was just what we needed as it had a hot shower. However, we would have to wait half an hour for the water to heat up, so we sat on his porch and had a beer and snacks. The snacks were different to any we had eaten in Nepal; it was bread, butter, cheese, nuts and dried fruit. He told us it was a typical Dutch snack. It made a welcome change and we washed it all down with a Tuberg beer. We got cleaned up and washed our underwear. It could have been quite embarrassing shitting yourself and having to get 'cleaned up' in front of each other, but because it was something we had both been subjected to, and we were both in the same sticky mess, it kind of smoothed over any awkwardness. I suppose it was a shared experience followed by shared embarrassment.

The lodge was very different. The Dutchman had two passions in life: astronomy and Clint Eastwood, hence the name of the lodge, High Plains Inn. Hanging on the wall of the dining room was a Clint-style hat, poncho and whip. It was a little weird, but no weirder than what Deb has in our back garden. She has collected two sheep skulls and put them on the gravel near the pond. Our local squirrels love them and often come down to nibble the horns. Why, I don't know, maybe they need the calcium? So we have two nibbled sheep skulls with moss growing out of the eye sockets. That's pretty weird. I would say it made the hat, poncho and whip seem pretty run-of-the-mill.

There was also evidence of the Dutchman's other

passion in the form of photographs of planets and nebula which hung on most of the walls. I was pretty impressed that he took these photos himself. If you are into stargazing, this is the place to be. The Himalayas is a dark sky area like no other. If it is a clear night, you can see millions and millions of stars. There is no light pollution from big cities and we saw the Milky Way many times during our trek. We stood outside one night when we were at Thorong Phedi, and even though we were freezing we just looked up in awe at the night sky in all its glory. It was one of those memories you never want to forget. It reminded me of the time we took the girls camping in Cornwall when they were younger. Grace our youngest, insisted I woke her up in the middle of the night to go outside and see the Milky Way. And that was another memory I never want to forget.

Our evening meal was also very different. We had Indonesian chicken skewers with fried rice, and apple fritters to finish. Then we sat by an open log fire and chatted to a Czech family who were staying there. The parents had walked the Annapurna Circuit 25 years ago. Now they were doing it again with all four of their children. Their ages ranged from 10 to 17. What a great trip to do as a family. It beats a beach holiday in Tenerife. But, I'm not sure all their kids would agree with that.

12

THE GUNS OF KALOPANI

The next morning we said our goodbyes to the Dutchman and his wife and set off on another day trekking. Today we were heading for Kalopani. It should be a relatively easy day today, as we are just following the river downstream for about 6 hours. However, I'm sure the heat will build up as the day progresses and that will add a strenuous element to test our resolve. First, we had to walk back along the road to the bridge we crossed yesterday. We felt very relaxed, our day's trek wasn't too far and it looked pretty straightforward; we had survived our tummy troubles and were feeling just fine, the sky was clear blue, and the breeze was gentle and warm. It's going to be a good day.

Our path took us through forests of pine and juniper, and the smells were fresh. There had been lots of recent landslides along the track that needed some careful negotiating, which occasionally required shuffling on our bums. We heard that locals use the landslides to slide logs cut from higher up in the forest, down to the valley floor. Once again the trail was very quiet, and we didn't meet any other walkers. This is the best sort of trekking. There was no one around, just us two on the trail, and the mighty Dhaulagiri loomed up ahead of us with its snowy peak pointing into the azure blue of the Himalayan sky. We could see the Dhaulagiri glacier; a river of ice slowly, but surely, flowing down the steep mountainside. Debbie told me that it is possible to trek to the glacier. It's quite an undertaking though, an 8 to 10-hour hike with an ascent of 1650 metres and then 1650 metres back down. That would be an extremely tough day, but it would have been a great excursion if we had had the energy. Maybe next time we come this way. Yes, I said next time, because I am sure we will come back to the Annapurna region again, it is just so beautiful.

It was nearly midday and we weren't sure what the temperature was, but it was hot. Kalopani wasn't too far away now, we just had to cross back over the river and then a short walk up the road and we would be there. The village is a long stretched-out settlement with most of the lodges and houses close to the one road that goes through it. We went into the Annapurna Lodge and enquired about a room. This was a large impressive building. It had more of a hotel feel to it rather than a lodge. The dining room had lots of polished wooden tables and large leather sofas scattered around. We both thought it might be a bit over our budget, but we were wrong. The price of the room was similar to all the others on the circuit. We booked in and ordered two beers, spring rolls and chips. We ate them outside and sat in the garden to cool off in the shade.

There were a group of about 25 German motorbikers also in the garden, with their dusty bikes all parked up. It is the only group of bikers we have seen. I can't imagine it would be too easy taking the kind of road bikes they had on the jeep road. They were all covered in dust as were their bikes, but judging by the loud chatter and laughter, they seemed to be enjoying themselves. After a couple of beers and an hour of relaxing in the garden, we went for a very civilised afternoon nap. Now I know this makes us seem like a couple of old grannies, but we had been trekking for 17 days now and our bodies needed a rest. So an afternoon snooze was perfect. It was marvellous just laying there with the window wide open and the sound of birds singing and insects doing their chirping thing. It was hard to believe it was November, and at home, it was probably cold and wet, but here it felt like summer was lingering on.

I awoke from my dozing and looked out of the window. I noticed a peculiar guy in the corner of the garden. The reason he looked strange was he was dressed in full camouflage gear and had an automatic rifle. I woke Deb up to come and look at the unusual guy, then we noticed others. There were about 6 of these soldiers around the outside of the building. We thought we had better go down and see what was happening. Also, our evening meal should be ready. When we had settled on a table, we asked one of the staff what was going on. He seemed very anxious and told us they were being visited by an important political official from Kathmandu. Our meal of dhal bhat arrived and so did the VIP. He was dressed in a very sharp-looking suit. He sat down on one of the large leather sofas and was immediately given a cup of coffee. His entourage of soldiers stood at various points around the room with their backs to the wall and still sported their lethal weapons. The lodge owner, who when we first met her seemed very confident and a little aloof, appeared to be cowed by the VIP's presence, maybe even frightened. It reminded me of the 'Godfather' films, where the gangsters had come to negotiate their protection money. Who knows, maybe that's exactly what was going on. Politics and corruption go hand in hand in Nepal, allegedly. Whatever was going on, it wasn't conducive to a relaxed meal. And it was the only place on the circuit where we weren't offered seconds of dhal bhat. I think the staff were a little preoccupied. We had coffee and tea and watched the show until we got bored. If this had been a scene from The Godfather, someone would have been shot by now. Or maybe the VIP kept them busy while someone put a yak's head in the lodge owner's bed.

The politician and his men were still here at breakfast, so they must have stayed here last night. We didn't hear gunshots in the night, so maybe their business went well. I suppose it was just another day at the office for them, and another day trekking for us. That's what's good about being a traveller, you float in and out of places and situations like an invisible ghost, observing while not being observed.

Packed and paid up, we started our walking for another day on the trail. This was to be a day of two halves. The first half was wonderful, but the second half was not so good. We hoped to reach Tatopani, but we didn't make it. We began by walking through the small village of Lete, where we bought our usual provisions for the day: Snickers, coconut biscuits and toilet roll. We can't go anywhere without these essentials, especially the toilet roll. The walking was good, and we passed through woods and farm yards. We crossed the Kali Gandhi on a small suspension bridge and walked into the very small village of Choyo. Here we turned right to follow a wonderful track that led us to another village called Jhipra Deurali. Direction finding was quite difficult at times and our guidebook suggested several different options. The option we decided on had a warning attached, 'Not suitable for people with a fear of heights'. Despite my reservations, we decided to go for it. We have read warnings similar to this one in other guidebooks only to find they're not so bad.

As I mentioned earlier, I used to be terrified of heights. The first time Deb and I went to the Lake District, we did a walk that traversed the side of a hill and reached a broad ridge that ran to the summit. On reaching the ridge the wind picked up and the exposure got to me. I had to hold Deb's hand and crouch down as we walked. We must have looked like Tarzan and his pet chimp, Cheater, and it was pathetic. But ask anyone who suffers from a fear of heights, and they will tell you when the fear hits, it hits. However, from this inauspicious start, I began to embrace the mountains and frequently pushed myself into situations of exposure to heights. I even did some scrambling and climbed Jack's Rake. This is a narrow track that winds its way up a near-vertical cliff face, with several places where you have to scramble over obstacles. It took me three attempts, but eventually, I made it. We took a selfie photo at the top and our faces were beaming with pride. I remember getting to the top and feeling euphoric. Since then we have done lots of other scrambles in the Lake District including Striding Edge and Sharp Edge, so we weren't going to be put off by the guidebook warning. So off we went.

We crossed a massive landslide and scrambled down the side of the steepest grassy slopes. This was very hard on our knees and our progress was very slow. There were some steps which had been cut out of the cliff face. It was a precarious path, one slip and you would fall hundreds of feet into the river below. Needless to say, we took it very carefully. The track took us down closer to the river then followed it along its bank as the path undulated up and down. It was sweltering again and we were starting to melt. Soon the path widened and we left the river behind. We didn't realise just how loud the river was until we walked away from it, and then the quiet took us by surprise. We had a rest in a shady spot and watched a family group harvesting a grain crop. They were using scythes and cutting it in the old way. All the family were involved, and the younger children were taking the sheaths and stacking them up. It looked like hard work and they must have been hotter than us.

We reached the small village of Pairothaplo and had a break for lunch. We sat in the shade while the owner made us a vegetable omelette and black tea. His young daughter, who was only 5, came to sit with us. She had a school book with pictures and English words. Deb enjoyed helping her with her pronunciation. She is great with kids and a natural teacher. I was too exhausted to join in. The heat had affected me, and my mood wasn't good. I couldn't cool off. There was no breeze and the humidity was very high. It took the guy 45 minutes to cook our lunch and, in my sullen state, I was complaining and moaning that we were running out of time to reach Tatopani. After we had eaten, I decided it would be too difficult to reach Tatopani and we would be best crossing the river and following the road back up the trail to the large village of Ghasa. This was a mistake and became the real turning point of the day. As I said, the first half of the day was great, the second half was hot, frustrating and more than a little ill-tempered.

We crossed the bridge and started up the dusty road to Ghasa. Jeeps and buses frequently rushed past us spewing great clouds of dust into our faces, which due to our wet, sweaty heads stuck to us and made us look like we'd worked a shift down a coal mine. On the outskirts of Ghasa is a bus station, and the whole area looks dirty and run down. This must be downtown, down-market Ghasa. We walked on and came across the Old Mustang guest house. We booked in, but we shouldn't have. It was a dive; it was dirty and didn't seem to be run very well. I was desperate just to get my pack off and cool down. Deb wanted to try somewhere else, but in my selfish bad temper, I said we're staying here. We ordered food and then went for a walk to cool off in the late afternoon air. I was still full of stress and badness. Then I launched into a real paddy and went off on a mega rant: "I fucking hate Nepal. Look at all the fucking donkey shit on the path. Why the fuck can't they sweep the shit up? I just want to go home. I want a hot shower, and be able to drink straight from the tap without fucking poisoning myself". I swear a lot when I'm angry. "I'm not fucking coming back to Nepal again, it's just one big fucking shit hole, and I can't wait to get home. I don't want to eat another fucking dhal bhat ever again. I want fish n fucking chips". All the while I'm having this paddy, I'm bashing my trekking poles into the ground. I would like to say at this point I don't have an excuse for this childish conduct, I just behaved like a spoilt kid having a tantrum. I would also add that Deb has the patience of a saint, and once my anger had been vented, I apologised over and over again. Back at the lodge, we had our meal of dhal bhat, and it tasted nothing like fish and chips. I think Deb found it hard to keep a straight face. Yep, once again I'm a hypocrite. I thought it best not to say anything, but I did enjoy the dhal bhat.

The couple we had met outside Ranipauwa, Ciaran and Helena, turned up looking dusty. They ordered food and came to join us. This was good for us, as we were a bit quiet with each other after my inappropriate, childish outburst. We played cards and showed them how to play Crash, a good Yorkshire card game. I had a beer, then another beer, then apple brandy, then one more beer and more apple brandy; I guess you could say I got pissed. It had been one of those days, and I know it wasn't a good idea to drink so much, but I did and I suffered for it later, which as my Dad would have said, "Serves you right for being such a bloody idiot." And, he would have been right.

I woke up the next day with a hangover from hell. But, I was determined to put yesterday behind us and make it up to Deb, who must be pretty fed up with me. I forced some porridge down and I put lots of honey on to help with the hangover. We said our farewells to Ciaran and Helena and hoped we would see them further on up the trail. Today we would get to Tatopani even if it killed me, and I would do it cheerfully and not moan once. I will wax lyrically about the scenery and wonderful countryside along our way. I WILL make amends.

Off we went. Deb was quiet, and I was fighting the urge to puke up. Luckily I managed to keep my breakfast down. Retracing our steps from yesterday, we crossed back over the river and headed for Pairothapla. The exercise was just what I needed; my head began to clear and I felt much better. We called into the same tea house we had been in the day before and had some black tea. Here we got out the guidebook and looked at what the path would be like today. Deb was beginning to come around; she never held a grudge for too long. I had a feeling this was going to be a good day. We drank our tea and then set off again. The trail was very similar to yesterday with lots of ups and downs and superb views. A little further down the trail, we came to the small settlement of Kopchepani. It is a pretty little village with lodges and a tea house. I couldn't believe it. It would have been better and quicker yesterday to press on and reach this village rather than going back to horrible Ghasa and the Old Mustang lodge. Ah well, it's no good having regrets; we did what we did, and on a positive note, if we hadn't gone back to Ghasa, we wouldn't have bumped into Ciaran and Helena again.

Our path was going downhill steadily now and we were losing altitude. It was noticeable that the flora around us was changing into more exotic plants and the heat and humidity were rising again. Soon we came to a bridge over the river and directly in front of us was the village of Dana. Our guidebook said this village was beautiful and well worth a visit, so we had a wander around. It was midday and very hot so most of the residents were indoors keeping cool, whereas we 'Mad Dogs and Englishmen' were out in the midday sun taking photos. It was a lovely village. The people who live here have taken real pride in their homes, and the place is clean and well-kept. There were flowers everywhere and wicker baskets full of different types of beans and grains drying in the sun, to be eaten in the bitter cold of winter.

I love the idea of harvesting produce in late summer when the energy of the sun has soaked into it, and then eating it in the depths of a dark winter to let the sun flood out again. At home, I make blackberry and elderberry wine. I pick the berries in August or September, and by November it is ready to bottle up. Drinking it, in front of a roaring fire, on a cold January night you can almost feel the heat of the summer, and it gives me a melancholic longing for the year gone by, at the same time as giving me a yearning for the spring yet to come. Yes, there's a lot to be said for preserving and bottling, and the people of rural Nepal are experts. It's not just about the practicalities of preserving food; it's about continuing life from one year into the next, which is what all living things are striving to do.

Having had a good look around the village, we walked

back to the bridge where we called into a tea house and ordered lunch. We sat in the shade and waited for our meal to be cooked. It gave us a chance to cool down. I needed to keep cool, as I have come to realise that the heat affects my mood. I'm sure there is a positive correlation between my core temperature and my stress levels, so staying cool is becoming more and more essential. I didn't want a repeat of the tantrum I had yesterday.

Crossing back over the bridge, we carried on. The next stop is Tatopani. I was particularly looking forward to the hot springs there. I love soaking in a hot tub, so the springs would be right up my street. We followed an old dirt road now, but there was no traffic on it so it wasn't too bad, and we passed through fields of vegetables and small clumps of woodland which gave us a little shade and a place to stop for a water break. Soon the track turned and steered us down to the river where we crossed to the main jeep track on the other side. There was no way around this, we had a 40-minute walk on this horrible road to get to Tatopani.

A bus came hurtling past us throwing up a cloud of dust. Thank God we had our buffs and glasses on. The bus stopped about 200 metres down the road and a young lad got off and ran back up the road towards us. As he got closer he started looking around on the road like he'd lost something. Then he picked up a chunk of something metal and ran back to the bus. We realised that the 'chunk' was a piece of the bus that had broken off while it was bouncing along the road. We hoped it wasn't a vital bit, like part of the braking system. We had heard of many bus crashes on these roads, and when you see the state of them and the speed at which the buses travel, it's not surprising.

Tatopani was a breath of fresh air. It was such a relief to get off that bloody, dusty road. We headed for the 'Dhaulagiri Lodge' as we had heard it had cottage-style rooms and a good path leading to the hot springs. The main street was bustling with lots of trekkers all buying trinkets and souvenirs. Tatopani is a crossroad for several other treks, hence the reason for the glut of trekkers. It is also on the jeep road which can be followed to Muktinath, so there are many Hindus and Buddhists in Tatopani who are making the pilgrimage to the Holy site.

We found our lodge and booked in. Our room was a chalet-style hut somewhat similar to the one we stayed in on our first night on the trek in Ngadi Bazaar. It also had a lovely garden where we had a drink and cooled off. I decided it would be wise to give the beer a miss and stick to the tea for now. I was itching to go to the hot springs, but Deb was unsure. I was happy to go for a dip in my undies, but Deb didn't fancy stripping to hers, and that was fair enough. My undies looked like swimming shorts, whereas Deb's just looked like undies. I grabbed a towel and we walked through the garden and down to a dirt road. We could see the entrance to the springs. It wasn't what I'd imagined it would be like. There were several concrete buildings including a bar and two mucky-looking changing rooms. We called at the bar and I paid my admission fee of 250 rupees and got Deb a milk tea. I went to the changing rooms and stripped down to my essentials. It felt a little strange walking out in just my underpants, but once I saw everyone else seemed to be in an assortment of knickers and budgie smugglers, I soon relaxed into it. The first thing I had to do, was shower off under a tap of cold water. So I got in the queue and waited my turn. I could see Deb at the bar taking photos. After the shower, I went to the hot pool where everyone was sitting around the outside. Some were sitting in the pool while others sat on the outside with their legs dangling in. I found a space and climbed in. It wasn't very deep, maybe just over half a metre, but my God, it was hot when I first got in, and it took a couple of minutes to get accustomed to the heat. I had heard some of these hot springs are more tepid than hot, but this one sure lived up to its name.

The reason these hot springs exist is that we are on the boundary between the Indian Tectonic Plate and the Eurasian Tectonic Plate which lies along the Himalayan Mountain range. 50 Million years ago the Indian Tectonic Plate moved northwards and collided with the Eurasian Plate. This caused the Himalayas to form when the rocks were pushed upwards. I still find it mind-boggling to think that, if you were to go to the top of Mount Everest and dig beneath the ice and snow into the rocks, you would discover fossils of sea creatures that lived in the ocean millions of years ago. This ocean bed was thrust upwards during the collision of the two plates and is still rising today by about 2 centimetres a year. It is at this boundary known as the Main Central Thrust boundary, that the immense forces produce heat. When water seeps down into the hot rocks below, it is heated, and when the water flows back to the surface it becomes what we call a hot spring. It's amazing to think, that because of an event that occurred 50 million years ago, I'm now able to sit in my underpants soaking my aching bones in a hot pool.

The people in the pool were a very diverse bunch. The guy opposite me looked Tibetan. His dark hair was long and tied back and he had an amazing moustache that hung down to his chest. He reminded me of a hybrid of Charles Bronson and Yul Brinner. There were young and old, male and female, eastern and western, a very eclectic collection of the human race. I wonder if this is what the United Nations assembly looks like, but without the very young of course, and maybe without sitting in their undies in a hot pool. Although maybe it should be more like this; all chilling out in the mother of all hot tubs. It could improve international relations no end; it's hard to start a war with someone when you are wearing a pair of budgie smugglers and drinking a can of Tuberg.

I would have stayed in longer if Deb had been with me, but I thought it best not to stay too long given what had happened yesterday, so I got out and dried off and we made our way back to the lodge, where Deb tried out the showers. They were also hot, so now we were both clean and refreshed. We decided to have a walk down the street to have a look around. The shops were typical of the shops we had seen on the circuit; stalls full of trinkets, walking gear and snacks. Inevitably another bracelet was bought. I'm going to have such a collection by the time we get home. Jean, my mother-in-law, will be calling me a hippy again, but that's okay, I probably am. There was a nice atmosphere here, everyone was happy and relaxed. Most seemed to be on a pilgrimage or starting or finishing a trek, so there was a relaxed excitement about the place.

We bumped into Natasha and Oleg, and she filled us in on their trek down here. She was in fine spirits, and as usual, she was holding court with a small group of people. She told us about her home in Russia and why we should visit St Petersburg. Deb put it on our list of 'places to visit'. Maybe that will be another excursion out of my comfort zone. Ciaran and Helena were also staying here and we sat together in the dining room. Deb went for the chicken sizzler and I went for the yak steak sizzler. You can hear these dishes coming before you see them. The loud sizzling makes everyone stop and look. Mine was still on fire when it was put down in front of me and I had to blow the flames out. It was delicious. We had been pretty much vegetarians going around the circuit, and that was fine. However, I felt we needed a boost of protein to repair our weary muscles, and this steak and chicken would do the trick. After several games of cards and a couple of beers, it was off to bed. I knew this was going to be a good day, and I was right, it had been.

13

GOING UP IN THE WORLD

It was another bright new day and we were ready to get trekking. Our aim over the next two days is to get to Gorepani. Some do this trek in one day, but we have decided to split the walk and have a one-night stop halfway at a village called Shikha. It would be a very tough walk to do it all in one go as it is all uphill, with a whopping 1670-metre height gain. In this heat, it would be madness. Also, Deb had a slight case of the runs. I hoped it wasn't the chicken sizzler from last night.

At the end of the village was the police check point so we went through the usual ritual stamping. Then we were off down the road for a short while before crossing the suspension bridge over the Kali Gandaki once again. On the other side, the only way was up, and up, and up. As we had been walking mostly downhill since Thorong La, this was a shock to the system, and the going felt very strenuous. A group of schoolchildren overtook us on the trail and offered to sell us some small oranges, which we eagerly bought from them. They looked very smart in their clean uniforms and as always they were keen to practice their English language skills, then off they went walking halfway up a mountain to go to school, and all with smiles on their faces. These children were proud to go to school and wanted to learn, they were very different from a lot of the kids we had taught.

I used to cycle to the school I worked at, and as I approached the school I would see kids waiting at the bus stop to catch the bus for just one stop. Just one stop! The distance was only a few hundred metres, but they still hopped on a bus. There they were at 8 a.m. eating crisps and Mars bars with their uniforms looking dishevelled and being so lazy that they couldn't walk even a short distance to school. We didn't see many overweight kids in Nepal, but about half of the kids in my classes were overweight or obese. I wonder why?

I never really liked school when I was a kid. Which is ironic since I ended up teaching for 22 years. I think it all started when I hit puberty, my face erupted into a thousand yellow topped hills, and my long hair became lank and greasy. I lost all my confidence and self-esteem. I reckon God has a wicked sense of humour; he develops your sexual equipment and sends your libido into overdrive, but at the same time he makes you look like you have a form of leprosy, so no girl within a hundred miles will ever fancy you. I used to envy the lads with a smooth complexion and an even smoother chatup line. They used to change their girlfriends more often than I changed my socks. This lack of confidence affected me at school; I couldn't look a girl in the eye let alone talk to one. It felt like I was destined to be a virgin all my life. You could say I felt sorry for myself, and you would be right. The only thing that kept me sane, was music and seeing my mates on evenings and weekends.

So it worked like this; I would go to school and have a hard time and be given homework; I wouldn't do the homework because I was so stressed and I couldn't face doing it, and I just wanted to see my mates; when the homework was due, I would play truant so I wouldn't have to face the teachers, who would also give me a hard time; I became pretty good at copying my Dad's handwriting and I would forge a note from him to explain my absence. I was in a vicious circle that spiralled out of control. This went on for a couple of years. I was pretty good at exams though, much to the disgust of some of my teachers, so I managed to stay in the top stream. At the end of the 4th year, which is now called Year 10, most of my year group left school to get jobs. Because I was in the top stream, I was expected to stay on and do my O-levels, the forerunner to GCSEs. Legally I could leave school, but I stayed on, but continued to play truant. How stupid was that! At some point, an official from the school board came round to our house and had a 'chat' with my parents and me. She gave me a straight choice; either come back to school and stop having time off, or leave and get a job. I left and got a job. Ten years of schooling and not a qualification to show for it. Wasn't I the clever one!

I worked at every kind of job there was. Woodwork machinist, line worker on a conveyor belt at Canada Dry, grave digger, landscaper, milkman. I didn't stay long in any one job, I got bored easily. The job I had for the shortest time was in a laundry. I was labouring, just lifting and carrying loads of laundry. The concrete floor was awash with water, and I didn't have wellies, and the women there were filthy-minded bitches; they thought it was great fun to tease this new 16-year-old lad and grab his bits when he walked past. I stuck it for 2 hours until break time, and then I made a break for it and never went back. Two hours has got to be some kind of a record. This process of chopping and changing jobs was also interspersed with periods of unemployment. I tried to time this to coincide with summer. I would work in the winter and relax in the summertime. I was probably the only semi-retired teenager in the country.

This continued until I started my relationship with Deb. It was before we were married and we wanted a car. I passed my test and landed my best job to date; I became a milk roundsman. Up to this point when filling in forms, and it asked for occupation I would put 'Labourer'. I was going up in the world now I could put 'Milk Roundsman'. I did the job for about three years, and we did get a car. This opened up a wonderful chapter in our lives. After work and in the holidays, Deb and I would drive into the Yorkshire Dales. We must have been down nearly every road in the National Park, and we loved it. It became our sanctuary away from the realities of life. Sometime later we got married, and we had George our first child. The pressure was now on. I had a spell at being self-employed and tried to make a business selling novelty pictures. I would buy picture frames, and pictures, frame them up and sell them around the shops. I am no salesman, and soon my venture failed.

My next job was as an insurance agent. The best thing about working for this company was after I had worked for them for a year I would qualify for a mortgage. This was important to us, as we were living in a council house and we didn't want George growing up in this environment. We wanted something better for him. It worked, and after I'd been there a year we bought our three-bedroom semi, and we had Tom, child number 2. The pressure was starting to ramp up now. Being an insurance agent only really paid well if you were selling lots of new insurance policies, and as I've already said, I am not much of a salesman. Times became hard, and it was a struggle to make ends meet and pay the mortgage. My father-in-law threw us a lifeline; he was a manager at a large manufacturer in Leeds. They were a subcontractor of Rolls Royce and made aerofoil blades for jet engines. Brian, my father-in-law, helped me get a semi-skilled job in his department. It was the best-paid job I had ever had. The only thing I didn't like was the shifts; as I mentioned earlier, they were punishing hours and I had to work the night shift every other week. Then there was the overtime which meant working weekends. Overtime one week would mean working 10 or 12-hour shifts. I couldn't keep this up until I retired, but I couldn't afford to stop. I felt trapped. What was I to do?

One of Deb's uncles had worked in engineering and changed careers to be a lecturer. I looked into it. I could become a teacher IF I had a degree and a teaching qualification. I had none of these, but maybe I could get them. I started studying with the Open University. Distance learning became my saviour, as I could work and at the same time get my qualifications. I enjoyed the studying and it went better than I had hoped; I even scored distinctions in several of my modules. I needed 360 points to get my degree in Physics, and at 60 points a year, it would take me 6 years.

It actually took me 5 years to get my degree and a further 18 months to get my Post Graduate Certificate in Education, and in September 1995 I got my first teaching post. I can't begin to tell you how good that felt; I went around for days with my chest puffed out. However, it didn't last. I had worked myself into the hardest and most stressful job I had ever had but by far the most rewarding.

I have no regrets about the way my varied career has gone. If I had stayed at school and got my qualifications, and perhaps gone to university, I wouldn't have met Deb, and as a consequence, not had my four lovely children. Also, the many different types of work I have done have allowed me to meet people from all walks of life and gain an insight into many aspects of life that I couldn't have had if I had gone down the more conventional route. I have been called lots of things in my life, but never conventional. My journey has made me a more rounded person and I am quite proud of taking the road less travelled; it's all been part of life's rich tapestry, and it has been a wonderful life.

We watched as the school kids disappeared over the ridge, and we turned to each other and said, "We're getting too old for this." Of course, we didn't mean it, just the opposite; we felt young and alive, and full of adventure. I like my sayings, and this is a favourite: 'You don't stop when you get older, you get older when you stop'. The secret is to just keep going and push yourself, even if it means, as I am learning, wandering out of your comfort zone.

We stopped for a tea break at a lovely little village called Ghara. Deb was still suffering from tummy troubles and we both hoped that this would settle down as the trekking was hard enough without the added difficulty of having the runs. The houses here were painted red and white in the Hindu style. It also had a school, maybe that's where the kids from earlier were going. As we were in no rush today, we had a long stop and admired the village, and watched the locals going about their daily chores. A lady was washing her small kids under the outside tap. It was one tap for the whole village, as there was no inside water supply. These kids are hardy washing outside in cold water. It is common to see the women washing clothes and dirty dishes outside under these taps and laying wet clothing out on walls and fences to dry. It's not an easy life. Their houses are very basic, and to our eyes, they look quite cluttered inside. They all seem to have an abundance of pots and pans of all shapes and sizes. If you were to compare their living space with a western one, you might conclude that they were not so clean, but some of that is because their dwellings are old and have walls of bare wood. Thousands of wood fires have darkened the wood over many years and also the daily acts of living life. They're not so much dirty, as lived in; and they display the patina of lives well-lived. The Nepalese are proud people who have no airs and graces, and they will welcome you into their homes and their hearts, you can't ask for more than that.

Fully refreshed and cooled off we set off up the hill again. Slow and steady, we were in no rush as we should arrive at Shikha for lunchtime. The tree covering was dense and we could hear monkeys calling out. Occasionally we would catch sight of them and try to take photos. It's not easy. They seem to know when you are just about to press the shutter, then they're off. It was a good excuse to stop and catch our breath though. There were so many stone steps and some were so high they made our knees ache. It was a relief to reach Shikha finally. The village is on two levels with a steep set of steps to reach the upper level. We had said we would meet Ciaran and Helena at a lodge called Serendipity but we didn't see it so we assumed it was in the upper part of the village. We couldn't muster the energy to climb the steps, so we stayed in a lodge in the lower part. It was called the Moonlight Lodge. We had some milk tea and settled in. There was a roof terrace to sit on which gave us a great view of the small village below.

Deb, who is a very keen gardener, eyed up the numerous vegetable patches and fancied a walk around to get a closer look. The village and gardens were criss-crossed with narrow paths, so we just followed our noses and explored. This was very relaxing and it was lovely to see Deb get excited about the things growing, and making plans about what she would grow next season. There were quite a lot of young children playing games, and we noticed a small group of boys playing with a makeshift bow and arrow. We got a little closer to see what they were firing at and discovered they were trying to skewer a cat. We tried to dissuade them from tormenting the cat, and I think we succeeded, but for how long, who knows? They were only about 9 years old, so they had a lot to learn. It was a lesson I learned when I was about 18 years old.

I acquired an air rifle. I can't remember how I got it, but I suspect I swapped a couple of LPs for it. My mate John Naylor and I decided we were going to hunt rabbits. Why the hell we were going to do that, I'll never know. We went down to a place near our local canal where we had seen lots of rabbits. There they were, and like all the best hunters, we crept up to them from downwind on our bellies. We got as close as we dared without spooking them. It was my gun so I went first. I aimed at a likely-looking rabbit and squeezed the trigger. I got it! The rest of the rabbits scattered and we ran to see the dead rabbit. But it wasn't dead. It was very much alive. It was leaping into the air and squealing in agony. I never knew rabbits could make a noise like that. We panicked. What the hell can we do? John suggested shooting it again, so I cocked the gun and loaded another pellet. I shot it again, and it started leaping and squealing even louder. I hit it with the butt of the rifle. It stopped moving and lay dead in the grass. We were both trembling with the shock and vowed we would never, ever do that again. I got rid of the gun. I can't remember how I got rid of it, but I suspect I swapped it for a couple of LPs. Another life lesson learned.

Back at the lodge we took some tea onto the roof and kept a lookout for Ciaran and Helena. We watched village life from high on our lookout post. Life rolls on at a very slow pace here. No one seems to rush around. The Nepalese have another saying, 'Slowly, slowly'. I could do with some of that philosophy in my life. It's not that they don't work hard, because they do, it's just that they mindfully pace their days. And that's another buzzword these days, 'Mindfulness'. This word originated from Buddhism. It was the teachings of Buddha that required devotees to practice meditation or mindfulness, and through this acquire enlightenment, and reach Nirvana, a task that can take a lifetime, and even then not be achieved. I need to say that this is a very simplified explanation of this aspect of Buddhism. The modern idea of mindfulness, practised in the West, is best described as an add-on to a busy life, something to pick up and put down when needed; it's a method of meditation to relax and calm a person down but without the need for religious and indeed spiritual aspects. Although, I am sure many practitioners of mindfulness gain spiritual sustenance from its practice. For me, I find when I am involved in a task, whatever it may be, I try to keep my mind on the task, and not let thoughts push in that might distract me or take me to a different place. But, that's easier said than done; I am pretty rubbish at mindfulness. I don't think I will achieve Nirvana any time soon.

Ciaran and Helena spotted us on the roof and booked into the lodge. They have embraced the Nepalese philosophy of 'slowly, slowly' better than we have, and trek at a much slower pace, and that's not a bad thing. We all shared a meal and played cards over a couple of beers. They're an interesting couple. I would say they are both around thirty, and they are both language interpreters. Ciaran is from Northern Ireland and translates the Gaelic and English languages, and Helena is from Paris and translates English and French language. They both live in Belfast now. It's been good spending time with them, and they are such good company. They are going up to Ghorepani tomorrow, as are we, so we will have a couple more days together.

We went to the loo before going to bed. I went first. At the side of the toilet was a gigantic spider. It was blue, white and grey and was the size of a dinner plate. It was even bigger and more intimidating than the one we encountered earlier on the Circuit. It didn't move. It just posed on the wall like a malevolent presence. I'm sure it was saying to me 'Come and have a go if you think you're hard enough'. I wasn't hard enough, and when I'd finished with my call of nature, I backed out of the toilet. I had to tell Deb before she went in. She had a look of horror on her face. This is an expression I don't see too often, as she is a very gutsy lady, but she said, "Spider or no spider, I really have to go, will you come in with me?"

We've been together for a long time and seen everything there is to see, so it wasn't a problem. The toilet was a quite small space, but I squeezed in with her. Deb's voice was strained with panic, and I knew I had to keep her calm, so I tried to make small talk about our day on the trek. I thought in the circumstances it was the appropriate thing to do, since it might cover up the embarrassment of the sounds and smells emanating from Deb's backside.

"Just shut up and keep your eye on the spider," she snapped.

Well, that didn't work, so I thought I would try shutting up and keeping my eye on the spider. Job done, we both backed out of the toilet, much to the amusement of the guy standing on the terrace having a sly cigarette.

Now Deb's bowels weren't happy and she needed several trips to the toilet during that very long night. And I do mean a very, very, long night. Of course, I did the gentlemanly thing and accompanied her each time like a good husband. This served two very good purposes: it prevented Deb from being attacked and bitten by the monster spider and increased my Brownie points tenfold. I needed the points as the memory of my tantrum had not completely faded away.

Morning came, and the spider had scuttled away to sleep it off. No doubt it would be refreshed for the next set of soft dolly trekkers to arrive.

14

POON HILL, BEARS AND POOL

It was the 10 of November and day 21 of our trek, we're heading for Ghorepani today. The meaning of Ghorepani is 'horse water' and the village was once used as a watering hole for the horse caravans and traders that travelled between Pokhara and the Mustang region. It was going to be a day very similar to yesterday; a short day but lots of steps going up another 815 metres, and it was also going to be a hot day again. We have heard that there aren't many lodges on the trek today, so we have topped our water bottles up and have some dried fruits, nuts and oranges, and as always, we have a couple of Snickers for our 'emergency rations'.

Our walk took us through the tropical jungle and up the usual million steps. The sounds of the animals and insects in the trees were wonderful to listen to, and we walked in silence much of the way so we could hear them. The small village of Phalate was a welcome sight and we found a lodge that would make us a pot of black tea. There was a small school here and the children were making their way to class.

Today felt very much like a re-run of yesterday, but that was just fine by me. I love this area.

We arrived in Ghorepani at midday. Again it was very busy and bustling with lots of trekkers. There were many stalls selling the usual stuff, and irresistible to magpies like us. We thought we would find a lodge then explore the village in detail and browse the stalls. Maybe I could treat myself to a new bracelet? I have to control my urges to acquire more bling.

We booked into the hotel Superview, and it lived up to its name. The view from the front of the hotel, and also from our room, was superb. We could see right down the valley we had walked up over the last two days, and also over to the Dhaulagiri Mountain range. It took our breath away. Ciaran and Helena walked up the hill and saw us having our lunch. We left them to settle in and went to explore.

Looking around the shops I saw something I needed badly: a small pair of scissors. My hair was getting a bit long, but that was okay. My beard was getting long and that was also okay. But my moustache was long and it had become what Deb would call a 'soup sweeper', and it was annoying. I couldn't eat or drink anything without making a mess of myself. It had to be trimmed. The scissors were a very cheap pair but they did the job, and I wouldn't be sweeping the soup for the rest of the trip.

The village was very touristy and had lots of hotels and lodges. It even had a music bar with a pool table, which we said we would call in before we left. We did buy a bracelet, but not for me. The next day would be Helena's birthday, and we wanted to get her a gift.

One of the bonuses of trekking is the ability to eat whatever you want without putting on weight, and we took full advantage of this. Most of the cafes had delicious-looking apple pies so we just had to sample them all. And, yes they were delicious. We are becoming quite the expert tasters of apple pies; maybe Mr Kipling could give us a job as quality controllers, or perhaps we could judge the apple pie competitions at summer fairs.

The hotel was great, and it was full. The dining area was enormous and full of people talking far too loudly. There was a fair share of red and yellow trousers on show which came as no surprise, as they seemed to be talking the loudest. It must come with colour; as soon as you put them on, the volume of your voice increases by 50 decibels. Natasha and Oleg were also there. Oleg looked more than ever like a fish out of water. He sat on his own looking menacing while Natasha had a chat with us. She told us about the trek up to Poon Hill. She had done it before and had gone up there for sunrise, but she advised against this. She said there would be hundreds of walkers up there and it would feel like a circus, it would be better to go up when the crowds had come down. That sounded like perfect sense to us, so we planned to go up in the morning, but after the masses had come down. Poon Hill is a special place for us and it was important for us to visit it whilst on this trip. This was because Tom, our son, and his friend John had been there; they tried to trek the Annapurna Circuit two years previous. They did the trek in January and only got as far as Upper Pisang and got snowed in. The British Army also had a group trying to get around the Circuit and they also couldn't get beyond Upper Pisang. If the British Army couldn't get through, what chance did they have? Instead, they got a jeep over to Ghandruk and trekked to the Annapurna Base Camp. From there they did the trek to Poon Hill. In his house, he proudly displays a photograph of himself at the Base Camp. So getting to Poon Hill had an emotional attachment to us, but we didn't want to be up there with the crowds of other trekkers.

When he came home and told us of his adventures, how wonderful Nepal was, and how friendly the Nepalese people were, it planted a seed inside us that is just coming into flower now. I always thought our children would walk in our footsteps, but we seem to end up walking in theirs. Our kids are such an inspiration to us both.

Abby, our eldest daughter, made a solo trip to tour New Zealand. We were so proud of her. It takes real courage to go off travelling on your own, but she did it. Tom went to Vietnam to teach English for two years, and we visited him for a couple of weeks; we all did a short trip to Cambodia, with George, our eldest, and his girlfriend Alex for an Oxley adventure. George had an adventure in our country when he moved to Scotland and forged a career in hospitality. He and Alex also had an exciting winter adventure in Iceland. One memorable trip we made was to visit our youngest daughter Grace when she travelled to Whistler in Canada for a year; she wanted to get some work experience and learn to ski in the winter season. Again, we visited her, with Tom, and had another Oxley adventure.

During our trip to Canada, we travelled over to Vancouver Island where we did some kayaking and saw the bears. Whistler was also an amazing place to visit. The bears sometimes wandered into town, and this caused problems for bears and humans alike. It's a bit of a dilemma, wild animals living amongst us. For lots of creatures, it works fine. If we saw a rabbit on our lawn, we would probably enjoy the visit, but what about if a black bear wandered into our garden, or down our local high street? Then I think we would feel differently. The police in Whistler have a policy for dealing with bears. It's two strikes and you're out. The first time a bear comes into town, it is tranquillised and tagged then taken back into the forest. If it comes in again it is put to sleep. Which is a soft way of saying it is killed. It's a hard choice. But, if a bear gets used to coming into town, it would just be a matter of time before it would hurt someone.

One particular evening, I was walking into town, and there was a commotion in front of me. It was a young black bear. It wasn't fully grown, but it was still a fearsome sight on the path. The group in front of me stopped walking and waited to see which way the bear would go. A police van pulled up and two officers got out. They both carried rifles. The bear fled into some trees and climbed up into the top branches. The crowd turned from, what first appeared to be, ordinary, nice people into an aggressive mob. One half was encouraging the police to "Blow its goddam head off!"

While the other half was shouting at the police "Leave it alone you murderers."

The officers were completely professional and explained to the crowd that they were firing tranquilliser darts and that the bear would not be harmed. (Unless of course it had already been tagged). But the crowd were all fired up now and continued to heckle the policemen. The thing I took away from the incident was, that people are not always what they seem and a mob can quickly turn nasty. Also, human beings need to come up with strategies that will allow us to live with, and cherish the wild creatures we share our planet with. Black bears are usually not aggressive, as long as you don't come between a mother and her cub.

There are also grizzly bears near Whistler and they are a completely different kettle of fish. They can be very aggressive and are definitely to be avoided. We asked a local lady how we should deal with a grizzly if we came face to face with one. She told us that you can't outrun a grizzly, and it's no good climbing a tree as they can climb up as well. She also said, "DO NOT PLAY DEAD. If you do, the bear will just maul you." We were glued to her every word as she continued her advice, "The best way of having a chance of escaping with your life, is to make yourself look as big as you can by lifting your arms above your head and making as much noise as possible. If there are rocks nearby throw them at it."

Bears are super scary beasts. The thought of trying to face down a fully grown grizzly bear is simply terrifying. I hope we never bump into one.

Yes, our children have led us on a merry dance around the world. I guess you could say we are both very proud of all our kids, and we're happy to follow their lead. It has been said that: 'The young can learn from the old' and I would agree with that, but I also say: 'The old can learn a lot from the young'. And that is a good thing.

I awoke in the early hours of the morning and could hear voices outside and the clickety-clack of trekking poles on the flags. Looking out of the window, I saw an amazing sight, and I woke Deb up to come and look. It was pitch black except for the illuminated snakes that were converging on the path that ran past our hotel. There were hundreds of walkers all with head torches and trekking poles heading up to Poon Hill for sunrise. We watched for ten minutes, and it didn't seem the lines were ever going to end, so we went back to bed.

We got up at about 6:15, and set off up to Poon Hill. The sun was up now and we could feel its heat when we walked out. But where the ground was still in the shade there was ice and frost, so we had to take care walking. It was a beautiful morning and so quiet. It seemed like everyone was on top of Poon Hill and we had the path to ourselves. It is quite a hike to the top; Ghorepani is at an altitude of 2860 metres and Poon Hill is 3210 metres so that's a climb up the steps of 350 metres. It certainly woke us up. As we started climbing up, hundreds of trekkers were coming down, and by the time we got to the top, there were only two people left up there; it was Ciaran and Helena. All four of us spent a good hour on top of the hill taking photos. It was Helena's birthday, so we sang Happy Birthday to her. She didn't have a cake, however, she did have an energy bar which she divided up between us.

The panoramic views from Poon Hill are magnificent. You can see across the Dhaulagiri Mountain range, Machapuchare and the Annapurnas. The Machapuchare Mountain is also known as the Fishtail Mountain because of its distinctive double summit shape that resembles a fish's tail. It is said that no one has summited this mountain and no permits are given to climbers wanting to climb it. It is believed to be the home of the god Shiva and therefore a sacred mountain in Nepal. A British team of climbers attempted to climb the mountain in 1957. They climbed to within 50 metres of the summit, but would not go all the way to the top, as the King of Nepal had asked them to respect Hindu religion. However, a New Zealander called Bill Denz climbed several mountain peaks without gaining permission. He climbed alone and it is believed he attempted Machapuchare. Did he summit? No one knows, and he took his secret to the grave when he was killed in an avalanche in 1983 on the slopes of Manaslu. So Fishtail Mountain is said to be the least visited place on the Earth; but not the least photographed.

Deb is a real mountain fanatic, she was in seventh heaven, and she took many photos. I think she would have stayed there all day, but we were all getting hungry as we hadn't had any breakfast yet. We made our way down back to the hotel and we all ate breakfast together. Deb and I had decided we were going to have an extra day here. Our hotel was a great place to stay and we had spare time, so it would be good to have a 'day off'. Ciaran and Helena were moving on today. They wanted to finish the circuit and were going straight to Ghandruk today. That meant they would finish at Nayapul the day after. After this, they had planned to go to India to do some more trekking. These two are an intrepid couple. We said our final goodbyes and swapped email addresses. Then off they went. It felt sad to be saying goodbye to them as they had become very good friends. We both felt deflated after they left and it took a while to shake that feeling off.

We had a day to wander the fascinating streets and alleys of Ghorepani. We thought we would start with a little gift shopping. So we wandered around the trinket and souvenir stalls. We bought some bits and pieces but nothing too large or heavy as we still had some days left to trek. Of course, any shopping trip has to include a couple of coffee stops. Ghorepani is well set up for catering to the tourist trade and the coffee was great, as were the apple pies.

We watched some of the local young men playing a game that looked a bit like 'shove ha'penny'. It looked like a fair amount of money was changing hands and their emotions were running high. It reminded me of the gambling games we used to play in my first job when I left school. I was employed as a woodworker and machinist. I worked for a small company making gates and pasting tables. It was a very small company, and there were only about ten of us working there. We were all lads between 15 and 18 years old. It was a very low-paid job. My gross pay was £5.50. That worked out at about 14 pence an hour. This wage was so low, that I didn't earn enough to pay tax. I did, however, have to pay my National Insurance stamp, which was 53 pence. So my take-home pay was £4.97, of which my Mum took £3 for my board, which left me with £1.97 for myself. Now I know you're thinking that this was probably not a bad wage for 1972. You're mistaken. To quote the woman at the Employment Exchange: "That is just slave labour." And she was right, it was.

Gambling was a daily practice here, and we would gamble on anything and everything. One exciting activity was the hanging bet. Several of us would hang from a ceiling girder, the winner was the last one hanging. Of course, there were also side bets being placed. Card games were another way of gambling. It wasn't poker we used to play, it was a game called Montana Red Dog. Without going into details of how it was played, it involved a pot of money which there was always a chance of winning, if you had the right cards that is. The game could get quite heated, especially when the pot of money grew large. No one ever lost too much and no one ever made much either, but it served as a distraction. Without this distraction we would probably all have left and got proper jobs that paid better wages.

It was a memorable time. The restroom was plastered on every wall with pictures of naked women, and we would sit on old dirty chairs and sofas, playing cards with more dirt on them than a gravedigger spade. Not many worked there once they hit eighteen, as other jobs would pay more. For me, it was an inauspicious start to a work career that would see me slowly rise to better things. We left the Nepalese lads to their gambling and wandered back to the hotel for lunch.

After lunch, it was time for a game of pool. I couldn't believe we were in a village in the foothills of the Himalayas and we were playing pool. How in God's name did they get a pool table up the mountain? I had no idea, but I'm glad they did. It wasn't the best pool table we had ever played on. It is fair to say it had been well used over the years with several strips of silver gaffer tape covering what must have been rips in the green felt. The overhead light was a small bulb hanging down on a couple of frayed wires. On the plus side, all the balls were there and it was free. It was advertised as a music bar and it didn't disappoint. We got ourselves a beer and started our first game to the sound of the Eagles and 'Hotel California'. We have played pool many times and in many places over the years, but this has been the most memorable of them all, and we'll remember it forever. I won 4 games to nil, but I think that was because I was luckier with the lighting. It would flicker on and off during a game, and it was off more than on when Deb was taking her turn. Deb is very competitive and usually wins at most games we play, so it was good to get the bragging rights for this match. The hard trekking over the last three weeks, and the beers over the last couple of hours, had the inevitable effect, and like a couple of old fogies, we went for an afternoon nap.

The rest of the day was spent washing clothes and pottering about. We got a bit bored and regretted having a day's rest. It was as if we had lost momentum. I know this sounds ridiculous, but that's how it made us feel, trekking every day over a prolonged period gets under your skin; it becomes a habit, almost an addiction, and very hard to break. I think we have become trekking junkies. Maybe we should have followed Ciaran and Helena's example and trekked on to India, or maybe over to the Everest region.

15

STEPS, AMERICANS AND DIZZY SPELLS

The next morning we couldn't wait to get our packs on and get trekking. We planned to walk to Tadopani. We had heard there were a lot of ascents and descents, so it was probably going to be another tough day, but that was okay, after our day of stagnation we were ready for the challenge. The first part of our walk took us steeply up through a rhododendron forest, and we had the company on our trek of a small dog. I tried to discourage it from following, but it wanted to come with us. There are lots of dogs in Nepal, and unlike dogs in the UK, they just seem to be left to get on with life. Nobody takes them for a walk, and they seem to spend most of the time lying around in the dust outside. I think that's why they tag along with trekkers, they enjoy going for a walk. I suppose dogs are natural trekkers and they are only doing what nature intended. They are, except for the dogs outside Chame, very friendly and affectionate, and they enjoy a bit of fuss being made of them. Perhaps this is because the Nepalese see their dogs as working animals and not pets, so a little bit of attention goes a long way with them. I think most of the dogs are kept as guard dogs. I'm not sure what breed a lot of the dogs are; they are quite large and stocky with a mixed black and light brown coat, a little like Rottweilers with longer fur. They look very hardy kind of dogs that could cope with the cold Himalayan winters. It is nearly the middle of November, and even at these lower altitudes, the weather seems to be turning colder. The early mornings were frosty and once the sun went down in the evenings, it felt noticeably colder. The dogs are going to need their thick coats in the coming winter months.

It was a slog up to the ridge, but it was well worth it for the view. The views were as good as the views from Poon Hill, and a good place to have a drink and cool down a little. We never tire of staring at the high mountains with their snowy tops. Deb likes to see if she can make out good climbing routes up them. She makes it sound so easy. I just cannot imagine climbing that high. Thorong La, at 5416 metres was exhausting enough. I couldn't imagine what it must be like climbing Everest. That must be one of the ultimate challenges. I know there are much harder mountains to climb, but Everest is the highest. I don't think I could ever have done it, even when I was younger. I'm sure Deb could have climbed it, if we could have afforded the massive cost involved that is.

I dragged Deb away from her mountain climbing daydream and we headed down the other side of the ridge to the tiny settlement of Deurali where we stopped for tea. There was a surprising amount of souvenirs on sale here for such a tiny place. Deb bought a new buff. It was a gold colour and suited her. I resisted another bracelet.

Tea drunk and Deb sporting her new gold buff we were

off again. We followed a path steeply down a narrow valley on hundreds of stone steps. Although it was hard on the knees, the jungle around us and the stream with its bridges took our minds off the pain. I love this type of path, you never know what's around the next corner and what wildlife you are going to encounter. After about an hour we came to Banthanti. We didn't want to stop as the tea houses were bursting with trekkers and after the peacefulness of the jungle path it all looked a bit too much. So on we went, onwards and still downwards. Once we reached the bottom of the valley, we had a stop, ate some nuts and had a drink. The next section was going to be challenging. For all the number of steps we had walked down, there was an equal amount to walk back up. We dug out our old mantra: 'Slow and steady' and started up the trail. We knew Tadopani was at the top of the ridge, but we also knew there were hundreds of steps to pull ourselves up before we reached it.

Eventually, we arrived in Tadopani, just another couple of red and sweaty trekkers. As soon as we got there we were drawn forward to the edge of what the guidebook called a balcony. The viewpoint here is fantastic. Annapurna South and Machapuchare seemed so close you could almost touch them. We had been walking for about 5 hours in the humidity and I was ready to call it a day. Deb thought we could do another 2 hours and get to Ghandruk. My expression spoke volumes, she read my face and it said, 'Not a bloody chance!' I wasn't going anywhere until morning.

Tadopani was heaving; it was like a Saturday afternoon in the centre of Leeds. Several treks cross here and there were lots of large groups. The first two lodges we approached were full. I was beginning to think maybe we will have to move onto Ghandruk after all. Finally, we tried the Himalayan Tourist Guest House, and they had one room left, so we took it. It wasn't the cleanest place we had stayed in, but it would have to do for one night. We had some lunch outside and admired the gorgeous view.

The table next to ours had four American girls on it. I had forgotten what make-up looked like on a girl. Apart from some lipstick, to protect their lips from the sun and the cold, dry winds, most women we had seen didn't bother with it. But these girls wouldn't have looked out of place in a cocktail bar in Manhattan. I think they must have been a little deaf though because they were speaking very loudly to each other, or maybe it was because they were wearing earphones and listening to music, if you could call it music. I could hear it from where I was sitting and it wasn't what I would call music. Oh God, I'm beginning to sound like my Dad! One of the girls was reading a book called 'Enlightenment'; or was it 'Enlightenment For Dummies', if it wasn't it should have been. They seemed completely oblivious to the environment around them and the awesome views of the mountains. Maybe if she had put her book down and looked at where she was, she really might have achieved some kind of enlightenment. Am I being a bit unfair? Am I judging these girls too harshly? Am I bollocks! They were loud and obnoxious and so I can justify my feelings of dislike for them without any guilt associated with it whatsoever. They were soon joined by four boys. They weren't wearing make-up, but I might have guessed it, they were wearing red and orange walking trousers. Yeah, I judged them right. As was our habit, we gave them a name. I wanted to call them the 'American Knob-heads', but Deb said I was being unkind, so we called them the 'Young Americans' instead. Now Deb might be able to moderate my language, but she can't moderate my thoughts, I will always think of them as the

'American Knob-heads'. I apologise to any other Americans who might be reading this. Americans, like all other races, are wonderful people. But we are all humans, and some of us fall far below standards fit for social interaction. These young people were in such a group as that. The fact that they were American is irrelevant, so I will just call them the 'Knob-heads'. And just to temper my observations, and in the spirit of fairness, I frequently judge myself to also be in the category of 'Knob-head' as well. Of course, they have the excuse of being young, but I have no such excuse. I guess you could say, 'There's no 'Knob-head' like an old 'Knob-head'.

The temperature dropped very quickly, and as it was nearly tea time we went inside to stake our claim in the dining room. The owner lit the stove and the room began to fill up with walkers from the large groups, and very soon it was packed. One of the guides asked us very politely if we would mind swapping seats with him so he could be with the group he was leading. We didn't mind too much, as long as it wasn't near the 'Knob-head' group. We sat next to an elderly German couple and their guide, and we ate our dhal bhat. Now I know what you're thinking: 'dhal bhat again!'. We like dhal bhat, and each lodge does it differently, especially the curry and the pickle bits. So in a way, it was like trying a new dish each time. And, you always get seconds. Except this time we didn't. The owner was so busy looking after the large groups we were left out. This is something we have noticed before. I suppose you can't blame the lodge owners for this, as it's the large guided groups that make them the most money and they need it to survive, so they have to keep them sweet. But, that's where the guide we were sat with came into its own. He went straight into the kitchen and brought out our second helpings himself. We thanked him and offered to buy him a beer, but he declined. The vast majority of Nepali people we have met have been so kind and are more than happy to help when they can.

We had a beer and played cards, then Deb said she had to go to the toilet. I carried on shuffling the cards when I heard a commotion. Looking up I could see Deb with a Nepalese guy holding her up. I rushed over to see what had happened and she said she had felt faint. The Nepalese guide wanted her to sit back down, I knew she needed fresh air so I took her outside into the cold night. This brought her around and she told me what had happened. She said she had felt like she was going to faint and tried to make it to the door. She didn't make it and hit her head and knee against a steel pillar. Bizarrely, she said when her head hit the pillar it made a strange noise like a cartoon would make: bbooooooygg! She was embarrassed and didn't want to go back into the dining room, so she went to our room and I collected our things. The people we had been sitting with were concerned, which was nice, until one of them suggested it was the beer, which was not nice and I became angry and told him, in no uncertain terms, that it was not the case. The guide thought it might be AMS and wanted to check on her, and I had to tell him it was not AMS as we were on our way down and that she was my wife and I was quite capable of looking after her without his help. I am afraid I became quite rude to these people. I was stressed out because I was worried about Deb and I resented any implications that it was the beer or that we were so incompetent to allow ourselves to become victims of AMS. I made it clear it was because the place was so warm and stuffy.

Another Nepalese guy gave me a plastic bag with ice to place on her head and I quickly went back to our room. Deb was upset. She was worried about what people would think, and I told her that I had reassured them it was just a dizzy spell brought on by the hot and airless room. She had a nasty bump on her head, and her knee was looking red and angry. I put the ice on her bumps to try and take the swelling down. As you can imagine, we didn't have the best night's sleep that night.

However, we woke to a beautiful fresh morning. Deb was very reluctant to go into the dining room, so I went in first to see how many people were in there. Most of the groups had made a very early start so the place was virtually empty. We went in and had our breakfast. The German couple came in and asked how Deb was. She said she was fine and that it was just too hot and stuffy last night. All was well and Deb was very relieved to set off and leave Tadopani behind. Whenever we look back to our adventure we always refer to this episode as her 'bboooyynng' moment.

The going was difficult again with lots and lots of steps and some of them very slippery. Deb's knee was sore from the knock she took, so we walked down pretty slowly. The glorious scenery around us helped to take her mind off the pain. We were walking in the tropical jungle again. I don't think I would like to do a jungle trek. The jungle around us was so thick and dense it would be hard to cut your way through with a machete, and in this heat and humidity, I'm sure it would be desperate. My Dad did his National Service in Malaya and trained there as a medic, and he probably did some jungle training whilst he was there. On discharge, he brought his machete home with him. I'm sure it was shiny back then, but when I used it to chop firewood as a kid, it was dull and its handle was blackened leather with copper rivets which were covered in green verdigris. I wonder how much chopping his way through jungles he did? I'll never know. I was a typical kid who wasn't interested in what my parents had done with their lives, and my Dad didn't speak about those times much either. And now he's long gone, and the memories of his life, that I would dearly love to hear, have gone forever. You never know how much you love someone until they have gone. I have very few regrets in my life, but I do regret not sitting down with my Dad more and asking about his adventures and memories. I miss him very much. I do try to tell my kids what I got up to in my younger days, although I am sure they will tell you I talk too much. We open our eyes to the great universe for the smallest of times, and then they close forever, so it is good to pass on our thoughts and experiences before they are lost to the darkness.

This was hard going. Sometimes the downhills are harder than the uphills and this is one of those times. We saw a clearing coming up and we were going to have a break when we realised the spot had been taken. It was the 'Knobheads' or to be polite, for Deb's sake, the 'Young Americans'. Aw, what the heck! The girls were all doing yoga. I'm all for people doing yoga, I wouldn't mind trying to get these old bones into it, but this wasn't the place to be doing the 'downward facing dog'. The lads were taking photos all except one, who was reading the 'Enlightenment' book. Needless to say, we didn't hang about and left the enlightened ones to their meditations.

We came across a lodge called The Lonely Planet and called in for some tea, and a sit down to cool off. The place was pretty full of large groups with their guides and porters. We wouldn't usually stop at a place this busy, but we needed a break from the constant downhill. It felt great to take our bags off. It wasn't too far to Ghandruk now so we could afford to take half an hour to have a drink, and of course, to people-watch. Judging by the numerous, different accents and languages, there must have been people here from dozens of countries; people from all four corners of the globe gathered here to experience this wonderful country. We overheard a guide talking to his group and he told them Ghandruk is only half an hour away, so off we went again.

Ghandruk is made up of two old villages, and it is one of the most beautiful places on the circuit. We had no problem finding the village, but some trekkers missed Ghandruk by going on the bypass path. Our advice would be not to bypass this place, as it has been one of our favourites. It has lots of steps and alleys to negotiate and it is very easy to get lost in its many backstreets, it is a wondrous place to explore. But, first, we had to find a lodge. There was so much choice, but we found a new-looking hotel at the top of the village. It was the Rodhee Hotel, and we were the only two people staying there. We had a lunch of veg fried rice and then set off to look around the village. It was no surprise to find a German bakery, and we called in for a drink and apple pie. The baker told us the apple pie was baking so we decided to stick with just a drink and call back when the pie was ready. It felt like we were kids again; my Mum used to bake pies and we would have to play out for half an hour to wait for it to cool down before we could try a slice. So we went out to play for a while.

We found the Ghandruk Museum, with its exhibits of Gurung culture, and had a good look around. We were fascinated by the many cooking pots. I wondered how many meals had been cooked in them. How many delicious dhal bhats had been served up to hungry workers after toiling in the fields all day? This was history on a plate.

We met an interesting lady, whose name was Helen. She was a spritely 80-year-old from Perth Australia. She had been coming to Nepal for many years doing charitable work with local children and women's clinics. I hope we are still coming into the mountains when we are 80 years old. I think I will be lucky if I do, as my body has too many problems. I saw Tom Jones on the TV a few days ago; it was his 80th birthday. I'll quote you one thing he said that resonated with me: "If I knew I would live this long, I would have taken better care of myself." We all get old, if we're lucky that is. It's then you start to realise that our bodies have so many inbuilt faults; design flaws that become more exposed as we get older. Take the prostate for example. For the first 50 years of your life, you're not even aware of its existence. After that, you are only too aware of its effect on your everyday life. Spines are another thing that also has a design fault. The vertebrae and discs undergo degeneration as we get older and then we're fucked. And don't get me started on arthritis and dementia. If I ever get to Heaven, and that is massive if, I'm going to have it out with God Almighty: "Come on God. I thought you were the big cheese. I thought you could do anything. What the hell were you thinking about when you designed a bloody prostate? Were you having a bad day? Did you have a hangover or something? Have YOU got a prostate? I'll bet you bloody well haven't. Typical! It's alright for you, but us plebs down here can like it or lump it. And lumps, that's another thing." You wait 'till I get to Heaven.

Anyway, Helen, the lovely 80-year-old, told us she had just heard that Donald Trump had been elected as President of the USA. Aw fuck! We're all going to hell in a handcart. He's about as enlightened as the 'American Knob-heads' I mean 'Young Americans'. She was as dumbfounded as we were; how in God's name did the American public get it so wrong? We met other Americans on our travels and they seemed genuinely embarrassed about their newly elected President.

We had played out for half an hour and now the apple pie was ready and cooled down enough to eat. We sat outside and enjoyed one of the best pies we had eaten, and looked around at the fantastic views. We were both feeling quite melancholy, as tomorrow was our last day on the circuit. I think both of us would have liked it to go on for longer. Still, we had one more day of trekking and then time in Pokhara and Kathmandu.

Back to the hotel for a hot shower and to order our tea. We had both decided to have chicken sizzlers. Because we were at the top of the village, and our room was on the first floor, the view from outside our room was brilliant, and we sat and watched the world go by. We saw the hotel owner go into his field and catch a chicken. To our surprise, he just wrung its neck in one quick clean action. He must have done it hundreds of times. Not to that particular chicken, of course, it was that chicken's first time, and sadly its last. Deb has higher sensibilities than I have and wasn't amused. She still enjoyed the meal though. Sizzlers are great, just don't touch the plate or it'll take your skin off.

The hotel might have been new, and it certainly was one of the best we had stayed in, but the rooms still didn't have heating, so we kept to our habit of sleeping in our sleeping bags. They have been a great investment, I don't think we could have managed without them. They were expensive, but they have been worth their weight in gold.

I woke up pretty early and Deb wasn't there. I got up and went to look for her. She was sat outside our room on the balcony with her sleeping bag wrapped around her. She had tears rolling down her face and said she just wanted to look at the mountains and take some last photos before we left them behind. It was a really special moment. I gave her a big hug and told her we would come back to the Himalayas again, and walk once more among the high mountains. And I meant it. We would be back. I would do anything for my Deb. I sat with her and looked at the mountains, and the mountains saw us and looked right back.

16

OUR LAST DAY TREKKING

After breakfast, we packed our bags and I had a coffee while Deb chatted to a Tibetan lady. She was on the porch of the hotel and had all her trinkets laid out on a sheet on the ground. The lady squatted and Deb knelt. They chatted away like women do. This is a wonderful quality that lots of women seem to have; they can talk to each other about anything and everything, and see other women as equals and part of the great body of womanhood. Maybe it would be a better world if more of our leaders were women. Kick out Trump, Putin and the Chinese leader Xi Jinping. Kick out Kim Jong-un as well, and replace them all with women. I'm sure there would be less conflict, and the world would be a better and safer place to bring children into.

Deb bought some small trinkets from the Tibetan lady and then we set off walking. Our last day on the Annapurna Circuit had arrived and today we would trek to Birethanti. The actual finish is about half an hour further on at Nayapul, but we would rather stay at Birethanti, as we have heard that Nayapul isn't the nicest of places. Then the day after we could stroll the last mile and catch the bus to Pokhara.

We slowly walked down through the village. The weather was once again superb with a bright blue sky. Today would see us walking down to much lower altitudes and we expected it to get very hot. The path left the village and Deb began looking for a side trail. She was very keen to find this track, but I was not. She had a diversion in mind that would extend our last day by quite a few miles. The path we were on was a good one and I was happy to continue on it. I think Deb was keen to make this day last as long as she could; she hated the thought that the Circuit was ending. While I was sad it was coming to an end, I didn't feel the need to prolong this last day, especially as I knew the temperature was going to increase to a thousand degrees and I was going to struggle to keep cool. And that's when it happened, we had our first argument of the whole adventure. We are a very close couple and we don't argue that often, but we are only human and on occasions, we have been known to disagree and fall out. Deb was angry that I didn't want to go on the side trek, and I was angry that she did. Fate intervened to resolve the situation, as the side trail was nowhere to be seen. After about an hour of giving each other the silent treatment, Deb apologised and we hugged it out and carried on our way.

The trail went down very steeply through fields of rice. The hillsides have been terraced so that rice and other crops can be grown. They plant rice in flooded fields, and once they are fully grown, they drain the field and this puts the rice plants under stress. Like all living things undergoing stress, they conform to one of the four Fs: Fight, Flight, Freeze or Procreate. Come on you can work it out. The rice procreates by producing seeds, or as we call it, grain. To build the vast expanse of terraces on these hillsides must have taken a monumental effort over many years. There was no way of telling how old they were, but I suspect hundreds if not thousands of years old.

As we walked down the hillside we came across a farm. Two women were sitting outside chopping wood, while a brood of hens pecked their way around looking for food in the dusty yard. We sat on a rock and watched this rural scene for a few moments while we had a drink of water. But this peaceful picture would soon turn to murder and abduction. A fox ran across the yard and past the women, who both had axes in their hands and grabbed a hen in its jaws. It made its exit on the other side of the yard. The women threw their axes at the fox, but to no avail, and the fox made its triumphant escape into the bushes. No doubt it enjoyed its ill-gotten gains with its litter of cubs. There is something about foxes that I admire. They are opportunists and are always ready to seize the moment whether it be stealing a chicken or scavenging a discarded slice of pizza. Foxes are survivors. But this was the fox's hunting ground and he was an apex predator. Would this fox be able to survive in the centre of Leeds?

Some years ago while walking the Coast to Coast long distance path, Deb and I stayed at a farm in the Lake District. We chatted to the farmer and he told us a tale of woe regarding foxes. He told us: "Some do-gooders rounded up nine foxes that were becoming a nuisance in the city, and released them here in Patterdale." He pointed to a small wood by the river and continued his tale. "Now foxes born and bred here, are very wary of us farmers and keep a low profile, but these stupid city foxes didn't have a clue." He continued "I shot five in one morning. They didn't move. They just stood there looking at me while I loaded up my shotgun and let 'em have it." He explained to us that every year he lost a fair few lambs to foxes. I don't think he enjoyed killing the foxes, but he had to protect his flock of sheep from them. The 'do-gooders' meant well, and they tried to do the right thing, but maybe they should have discussed the foxes' release with the farmer first.

The heat was starting to build now so we thought it would be a good idea to find a shady spot and sit down for a while. There was an old barn up ahead so we went to its shady side and took our packs off. We sat there a while and cooled off. Then Deb said, "Is it snowing?". I told her the sun is so hot it's cracking the flags, It can't be snowing. But, there were white flakes of something floating down from the clear blue sky. Then we both could smell the fire and began laughing. I had a similar experience about a hundred years ago when I was 14.

The main street where we lived was due to be developed, and all the old shops were closed and boarded up ready for demolition. This was a great playground for young lads. We would find a way into all the old Victorian properties and shops and explore and make dens. My younger brother Steve once kept pigeons in an old building for months. The old shops were the best because there was always 'stuff' left behind when they moved out. The bakery was a rich source of things to make mischief with. We found a massive bag of flour, took it up to the first-floor window, and waited for a victim. It wasn't long before we spied one coming down the main street. It was a boy who used to hang around with a bunch of lads who were older than we were. You know what lads are like; they were older so they used to push us around a bit. So when we saw this lad coming down the road hand in hand with his girlfriend, we could hardly contain our excitement. As they passed underneath the window, we let the bag go. Bullseye! They were covered from head to foot in flour, and we scarpered out of the back door of the building. We could hardly run as we were laughing so much. I don't think he ever found out who had done it, and we weren't going to tell him. Anyway, back to my experience of the mistaken snow.

It was December, just before we were due to break up for the Christmas holidays. My mate Kenny and I didn't fancy going to school, so we bunked off. We decided we would have to lay low, so none of our families would spot us playing truant, so we went into the old chemist shop. We had been in this place lots of times before. The way in was around the back of the building, and through a window on the first floor. To get up to it we had to climb up an old metal drainpipe. That was the only way in, and the only way out. The rooms were all boarded up so it was quite dark inside. We went into the attic where there was a dormer window so we could see better. Kenny had brought a board game to play, and while he was setting the game up, I collected some wood from around the building and lit a fire. It's a cold business playing truant in winter. Some old bits of broken chairs would burn well. There was no fireplace, so I built a fire on some tiles that I'd found in an old store cupboard. We soon had a good blaze going, but we were careful not to put too much wood on in case it got too big and someone saw the smoke. We played the game for a while until we became bored, then we went downstairs into the old shop and went looking for stuff that had been left in the old wooden drawers. Kenny looked out of the shop window through a gap in the boards; he thought he might see his Mum who sometimes came shopping down this way. Then he said, "Is it snowing?". It wasn't snowing, and there was a policeman on the other side of the road. We both knew exactly what the 'snow' was, and why the policeman was outside. We ran upstairs to the window exit, but when we looked down there was another policeman at the bottom of the drain pipe, but he didn't see us. We were in a real fix. What the hell were we going to do? The answer we stupidly came up with, was to hide. But where? In the cellar! We went down into the old cellar. It was dark down there, but a little light came in from the grating that opened out onto the pavement. We looked around for a hiding place or something to hide behind when we discovered a doorway. It didn't have a door in it but it led into a very dark and long cupboard. We inched our way into the pitch blackness and felt a stone table or long stone shelf. We both got under the table and waited. It was total darkness, we couldn't even see our hands in front of our eyes. We began to hear sirens outside and knew it was fire engines. The banging started. Our hope was, the fire brigade would put the fire out and then all go away so we could get out. We sat there hunched up on the ground scared to death of being discovered or worse still being burnt to death. Someone came down the steps, we could hear his footsteps and see the light from his torch. This was it, we were done for now. He didn't see the cupboard we were hiding in and we heard him go back up the stairs. Relieved we continued to wait it out. Time went by and we still didn't dare move. I remember my backside had lost all feeling and I felt I was going to pee myself, but we could still hear the firemen upstairs so we didn't move a muscle. Eventually, all went quiet, but still, we waited. I'm not sure how long we waited for but it seemed like ages.

We decided to move out of our hiding place and slowly go up and out of the cellar. The smell of burning was intense as we got out of the cellar and up the stairs. We looked out of the exit window and all was clear. We scrambled down the drain pipe and then ran and ran until we thought our lungs would burst. I have done some very stupid things in my life, but this has got to rank in the top three. Setting fire to a building and hiding in the cellar while a fire rages above you is a dumb thing to do. How I managed to survive my childhood I will never know.

Back on the trail, we carried on down through the farmlands and soon came to a small settlement. It was time for lunch, so we found a shady spot and ordered food. We got chatting to a Dutch guy. He was doing the circuit on his own and in a clockwise direction. He picked our brains about our experiences, and we expressed our concerns at his choice of direction and how risky it was doing it that way round because of the massive height gain from Muktinath. But hats off to the guy, doing an adventure on his own took lots of courage. We have met a few people on our travels that were alone and I always had great respect for them. I'm not sure I would have the bottle to do it solo. I don't think I would enjoy the experience as much either. It has been great sharing adventures with Deb and it has strengthened the already strong bonds between us. Couples who adventure together, stay together. Either that, or they kill each other. Which I think Deb has come close to doing several times over the last few weeks.

Lunch over, we wished the Dutch guy good luck and set off on the last leg. The next village would be Birethanti. There was a troop of monkeys near a large waterfall, so we stopped to watch them. They took off into the trees when they saw us coming. Deb had a bag of nuts, and she left them on a rock for them. It was another example of leaving food for the 'little creatures'. As we walked away we saw the monkeys come down to investigate what had been left on the rock. The big monkey, who we assumed was the alpha male, let out a loud howl. We both simultaneously said, "He was saying thank you." We loved seeing the monkeys. It was affirmation that we were in an exotic land, full of wonders.

We have seen quite a few swings on this leg of the circuit. They are made of bamboo and are very tall constructions. They are known as Dashain swings or 'pings'. These enormous swings are made of four very long pieces of bamboo strung together with natural rope, and the swing itself hangs down and provides the user with an impressively long arc of travel which can result in pretty high speeds. Dashain is a very important Hindu festival; it is a time when families reunite from across the country and party; they wear new clothes, feast, play music, dance, and play games. One of the children's favourite games is the Dashain swing No one was on this one and we couldn't resist having a swing. It doesn't matter how old you get, it's still good fun doing the things you did as a kid.

Birethanti was just up ahead. We crossed the river over the road bridge to enter the village. We walked across the bridge and approached the finish. It was only at that moment that I had noticed the lack of rain, and what superb walking weather we had experienced. I said to Deb, "We have carried our waterproof jackets and trousers around the Circuit, and it hasn't rained once. How lucky are we?"

There was a check post here and we did our final check-in. Now to look for a lodge. I had read in the guide book, that a good lodge here is one called Green Hill Lodge. Birethanti is a busy place, and we walked down the main street. We couldn't see the lodge anywhere, and we ended up walking so far that we reached the outskirts of Nayapul. We turned around and went back. I saw a likely-looking lodge and we asked about a room. He showed us the room and told us "The price of the room is 2000 rupees."

A Walk Among Giants

I laughed at him and said, "That's way too high."

He asked us "How much will I pay for the room?"

"500 rupees," I said, as this was the maximum we had paid on the entire trip.

He shook his head and said, "Not enough."

I wasn't too bothered, I had a bad feeling about this guy, there was something about him I didn't like. I told him "We will try somewhere else," and we started walking out.

He chased after us saying, "Okay 500 rupees."

I told him "You are too greedy and have missed your chance," and "2000 rupees is ridiculous."

I was in no mood to pull my punches, my core temperature was going through the roof and I just wanted to get my pack off and have a cold beer. We went right back to the beginning of the village where we first crossed the bridge. The lodge there was the Sunrise Hotel. We booked in.

The room was great and had a hot shower all for 500 rupees. After we cleaned up, we had a beer sat outside in the shade and watched the busy street. We had done it! We had completed the Annapurna Circuit, we did it without a guide or porters, completely independently. This beer should have been champagne, but who wants champagne when you can have beer? We drank to our success. Tomorrow we would walk the half hour to Nayapul and catch a bus to Pokhara. But for now, we could just relax, eat, and drink beer.

After our meal of chips and momos, the temperature started to drop, and it was now too cool to sit outside, so we moved into, what passes as a conservatory around these parts. To be honest, it was more like a heated greenhouse, but it was warm and comfortable and we were more than happy to while an hour away sat there. An old and scraggy-looking dog slipped through the door and into the room. It appeared a bit neglected and looked very sorry for itself.

Deb went into her bag and gave it a coconut biscuit. The dog was not supposed to be in here, and when it heard the owner coming to bring us another beer, it shuffled under our table and sat on Deb's feet. Needless to say, we didn't dob the dog in. We felt sorry for it and let it stay with us and eat Deb's biscuits. I did point out to Deb that I think I could see fleas moving in its fur, but she said, "After all we had been through, a few fleas won't hurt. Besides, I think he needs a bit of Debbie love." So the dog kept Deb's feet warm, and Deb kept the dog's tummy full. It's what is known as a symbiotic relationship, or you scratch my back, and I'll scratch yours. And I'm sure Deb will need her back scratching when the fleas get to work on her.

PART IV

A TALE OF TWO CITIES

17

A BUS, A MOUSE AND A PROSTATE

Morning arrived, and we started walking over to Nayapul. It felt a bit sad and strange to think our trek was over. I genuinely think if we had the time, we would have considered turning around and going back around the Circuit to Besisahar. But we wouldn't have time for that, so it's the bus to Pokhara for us. It's still sad though.

Nayapul had the feel of a miniature version of Kathmandu; it was dirty, smelly, and bustling and there appeared to be quite a lot of earthquake damage. We looked for a bus stand but couldn't find one, so we asked a young Nepalese guy and he guided us around a corner and pointed up the hill. It seems the bus doesn't come through the village anymore, it stops on the new main road. We walked up to the main road to find an old man there with a tiny tea stall. We asked if the bus stopped here and he told us it did. He made a living selling tea to people on the buses that pulled in, and he started to make us a cup of tea when the bus arrived. A young guy was hanging out of the door of the bus as it pulled in. He said it was going to Pokhara so we got on.

This bus was a type known as a 'local bus'. They look very old and battered and painted with every colour known to man. They have garlands and models of Hindu Gods hanging in the front window. They seat about 25 people, but they would think nothing of squashing many more inside or up on the roof. The two things that hit you when you get on are the smell and the noise. The smell is a combination of stale pee, exhaust fumes and incense sticks. The noise emanates from the sound system, on full blast, playing modern Nepali pop music.

We found seats near the back of the bus. The legroom was impossible and must have been made with very short people in mind. I just managed to squeeze in. I leaned back only to find the back of the seat had been bent to an impossible angle. I wouldn't be able to sit here for long before needing a good physiotherapist to sort my back out. I moved to another seat. That's when I noticed my backside was wet through. Bugger! What had I been sat in? I didn't want to touch it. I would just let it dry on its own. I hated that bus ride. The young guy came to collect our fare, which was so cheap: 150 rupees each. That's about 50 pence each for a three-hour trip.

The young conductor had taken a shine to me and sat down in the seat next to me. He was asking about where we came from and what we did for a living. He spoke very softly in very broken English and because the music was turned up to 11, I could hardly hear what he was saying. I didn't want to offend the guy, so I did my best to have a conversation with him. But I just wanted him to go away and let me suffer this bloody awful journey with my bad-tempered thoughts.

A couple of miles down the road an old man got on, and he sat in the seat in front of me. He looked pretty dirty, and he stank. It couldn't have smelled worse if a rotting zombie had sat in front of me. Somewhere in the forgotten recesses of my addled brain, a memory pushed its way into my consciousness. I was about nine or ten when this unfortunate incident happened. I was playing out with my mates one evening. I remember it was getting dusk, and I had been told to come home before it got dark. The street lights had come on, and we were playing in a cobbled yard. I can still clearly see the light reflected off the wet cobbles, and a tiny mouse running along in the gutter trying to get up onto the path. This was irresistible to young lads, and we rushed over to catch it. I was the quickest and cupped the little mouse in my hands. It wriggled around and tried to escape, but it couldn't get through my interlocked hands. It felt warm as it ran around inside my makeshift prison. I thought maybe I could take it home and keep it in a box in my bedroom. It would have to be a secret pet mouse though, as my mum would never allow a mouse into the house. I could get some mouse food from the local pet shop. My brother and I were always doing stuff like this. We've taken home: dogs, kittens, hedgehogs, baby birds and even a ferret. So I decided to take this mouse home. I would put it in a shoe box under my bed and keep it as my pet. For now, though, I would put it into my parka pocket. So I transferred the little mouse carefully from my hands to the inside of my pocket and closed the flap. Then I remembered I had a hole in my pocket. I put my hand inside and the mouse had gone. The question was: had it escaped from my pocket and run free, or into the lining of my coat? It was nearly dark now and I had to get home. Mum was pretty strict about this. But, I couldn't risk the mouse escaping from my coat into the house, as my mum would go ballistic. I had to be sure the mouse was not in the coat. So I took my coat off and laid it on the ground.

Then I jumped up and down on it like we did during PE at school. If the mouse was in there, it would be dead and couldn't infest our house. I ran home and thought no more about it. I had convinced myself that the mouse had probably escaped, mice are good at that. I've watched enough episodes of Tom and Jerry to know mice are slippery creatures capable of great feats of escape. It probably got out of my pocket without me noticing.

About a month later my brother Steve and I were on a bus with my mum and Aunty Irene. I sat next to Irene. She was quite a big woman and took up most of the bus seat. I was squashed up against the window. I wasn't happy at sitting with Irene, as she was my least favourite aunty and I got the feeling she didn't particularly like me. I wanted to sit next to my brother, but I don't think my mum and Irene would have fit onto a seat without one of them hanging over too far into the aisle of the bus and causing an obstruction. There's a two-fat ladies joke there somewhere, but it's probably best not to say anymore. All seemed to go well at first and I settled into the bus ride and looked out of the window. Then I got a sense of Irene's discomfort. She was restless and wouldn't sit still. Then she said, "There's a funny smell on this bus. Can anybody else smell it?".

I couldn't smell anything, but my mum agreed that there was a strange smell "Have you trodden in anything David?". Whenever there was a smell about, she always asked if we had trodden in anything. I assured her that my shoes were clean, but when we got home, the smell was still there; it had followed us from the bus. An investigation was activated and my mum told me to take off my coat. Irene sniffed the coat very enthusiastically like a bloodhound on the trail of an escaped convict, and then she took a pair of scissors and cut open the lining of my beloved parka. "Stop!" I shouted. I wasn't happy about this at all, I loved my parka. Mum joined in now and peeled back the lining to reveal the source of the smell. There it was, the little mouse, as flat as a pancake, and stinking to high heaven.

Irene had that smug look on her face and she said, "Boys are dirty horrible things."

She had a daughter, and they are made of sugar and spice no doubt. I wanted to ask Mum if I could have a new parka. But from the look of shame she had on her face at that moment, I thought it best not to ask just yet. I should have felt sorry for the little mouse, but I was too busy feeling sorry for myself.

So there I was, trying to decipher the conductor's gibberish, trying not to breathe in the fumes coming from the old guy in front, and all this while the driver pumped out the most hideous music I have ever heard at eardrum-damaging levels. Could things get any worse? Yes, they could! I am an older guy, and if I ever forget it, my prostate reminds me. Yes, I needed a pee. The questions were, how far was Pokhara? Could I hold out? If I asked the guy to stop, would I have to pee at the side of the road like some very young kid whose stressed parents can't get them to a toilet? I asked the guy how long to Pokhara. He said: "About half an hour". That was doable. If I stayed calm and tried to take my mind off peeing myself, I might just make it.

The smelly guy got off and the conductor went to hang out of the door. I turned inwards and mindfully tried to be aware of my breathing. Minutes later I heard the conductor shouting down the bus. This was our stop. Alleluia! We got our bags and scrambled to the front dodging the gas cylinders and live chickens. The conductor told us Lakeside was just down that road, and then the bus dodged back out into the stream of traffic and was gone.

We were left on the side of a very busy road and started walking towards Lakeside. By now my bladder had gone into a severe meltdown. If I didn't get to a toilet soon, the dam would burst. I didn't dare pee in the street. What were the decency rules in this country? If I were in Leeds City Centre, I might get away with it. Even if I was taken to court, I'm sure a letter from my doctor would be enough to get me off; also if the magistrate was an old guy, he would probably be able to empathise with me, but in Nepal, I'm not sure. I wouldn't want to be in a prison in Kathmandu. It would be like a scene from 'Midnight Express'; someone might bite my tongue out and I'd get raped by the large, sweaty, Turkish Governor. Sod that! I'll find a toilet, it's not worth the risk. We saw a cafe and while Deb ordered I used the facilities.

I emerged from the toilet with an expression of relief on my face. My mood had lifted and I sat drinking my coffee and began to forget the bus ride from hell. We later found out that we could have caught a taxi for about £12. Oh God, I need a beer. We walked down the very busy main road to Lakeside, and to the hotel we had left our luggage in. It seemed like such a long time since we had set off to Besisahar. However, there was no room at the inn; the hotel was full. They fetched our luggage from out of storage and left it behind reception while we went back into Lakeside to find a new hotel, which we did. It wasn't quite as good as our original hotel, but it was clean and cheaper. We retrieved our luggage and settled into our new home for the next few days. The first job was to shower and change into fresh, clean clothes. Wonderful! The next job was to ask reception if they could arrange flights for us back to Kathmandu. We didn't fancy another rollercoaster ride on the Prithi Highway to Hell. The guy in reception was most helpful and organ-

A Walk Among Giants

ised this for us. So the plan was to stay here for four nights, then fly to Kathmandu, have three days there and then fly home. All this done, we went for a stroll along Phewa Lake and had a beer to help calm my frazzled head.

It's impossible to walk around the area of Phewa Lake without encountering the street food vendors. They were selling Nepali Chatpate. This is a cold dish they make to order in front of you. It has many ingredients all mixed and put into a cone to eat with your fingers. The ingredients are: crushed, dried, spicy noodles, spring onions, fresh chilli, puffed rice, coriander leaves and lots of other stuff, but I couldn't tell what it was. The sellers all had trollies with contraptions built onto them to hold small buckets with lots of ingredients in them. They would pick a selection and give them a good mixing before they emptied the mixture into your cone. It was fascinating to watch, and I couldn't resist trying some. I thought, if it makes me ill so be it, I have to try some street food before we go home. That said, it might have been safer to get something cooked and piping hot. Nevertheless, I gave it a try. It was moorish. It had crunch, flavour and plenty of chilli heat. I just hoped the girl who made it up for me, had washed her hands.

While we ate our snack, we looked over to the stunning view over the lake to the Peace Pagoda. Looking through our guidebook convinced us that we had to go up to it. To get to it we would have to cross Phewa Lake and then climb up to the top of the hill where the Pagoda is situated. The Peace Pagoda has a very interesting history to it. Nichidatsu Fujii, a Japanese Buddhist monk, met Mahatma Gandhi in 1931 and was so impressed by his ethos of non-violence, he devoted his life to the same ethos. In 1947 he was inspired to build numerous Peace Pagodas at different locations around the world to honour and remember all those killed in the atomic bomb attacks on Hiroshima and Nagasaki at the end of the Second World War. He hoped that they would become a symbol of peace and non-violence throughout the world.

The Pagoda in Pokhara was started in 1973, but many of the builders were arrested on false accusations, as the government at the time didn't want the Pagoda built. When the building reached 35 feet in height the government moved in and destroyed it for 'security reasons'. However, work on the construction continued in secret and in 1992 the foundation stone was re-laid and construction went ahead, without hindrance this time. The Pagoda was officially opened in 1999. Nichidatsu Fujii died in 1985 at the age of 99 years, so he never saw its completion. He was responsible for building 80 Peace Pagodas in total, most of them under his supervision. What a man, and what a legacy! Some might say he was naive to think he could do any good building Peace Pagodas. But I think it was a wonderful idea. There are so many tyrants and violent people in this world, but let us not forget that there are also many good people as well, and Mr Fujii was one of the good guys. What good does a pagoda do you may ask? It is a large, white structure that cannot be ignored and can be seen for miles around; it reminds people that the world would be a better place if we loved each other instead of killing each other. I believe, that sentiment, is one that the majority of the people in the world would agree with. God bless you, Mr Fujii, wherever you are now.

To get across the Lake we needed to hire a boat. This was difficult on this particular day, as it was a Hindu festival day, and crowds of people were getting on boats to get to the small island on the lake. Here there is a small temple called 'The Tal Barahi temple' and on festival days Hindu families come to place their offerings on it. We saw the queue and got in line. No sooner had we started to queue, than a young guy with a stripy T-shirt pulled us out of the queue and took us to the front. He told us the queue was just for pilgrims and not tourists. He sorted us out a ticket and took us to the lake where he quickly produced a rowing boat. We told him of our plans to visit the pagoda and he pointed out a landing place on the opposite shore of the lake.

It was so peaceful on the lake, so we took our time. There's something very relaxing about being on the water. Perhaps we should downsize now we're retired and buy a barge on our local canal. I don't think I'd get that one past Deb. The water was a light green colour and felt warm to the touch, so we just floated about for a while and let the world go by.

We found the landing point and tied our boat up. There were other boats here as well, but it felt a bit strange leaving it here unattended. Would it still be here when we got back? We set off walking up the hill on a zig-zag path. It was quite a steep walk to get to the top, but we eventually made it. The Peace Pagoda, at 110 feet high and painted brilliant white, was a very impressive sight. We had to take off our boots before climbing the steps to the Pagoda, and there were signs asking people to walk around in silence. Deb and I had no problem with that, but the hoards of young people and kids found it an impossible task. It was like being in the schoolyard. And it was no good being angry, we just had to accept it for what it was. The youngsters didn't mean any disrespect, they just acted like teenagers do. Though it would have been nice to experience the Peace Pagoda in peace, it wasn't to be. If we came this way again, we would make sure it was at a less busy time of day, and maybe not during a festival.

Rather than go straight back down to the boat, we thought we would explore along the top of the ridge. A little further along the ridge was a restaurant, so we went in for coffee and cake. After this, we wandered up to another small summit that was covered in hundreds of prayer flags all waving madly in the wind. The familiar colours of the prayer flags are seen everywhere in Nepal. There were thousands on Thorong La and every suspension bridge we had crossed, had prayer flags strewn along them. There is a lot of symbolism attached to the flags, they're not just for decoration.

The five colours are always placed in the same order and represent the natural elements: blue sky, white air, red fire, green water, and yellow earth. When these flags are together they represent natural balance. Written on the flags are prayers and blessings. I used to believe the flags were meant to carry prayers to the gods, but I was wrong, this is not the purpose of the flags. It is said the flags purify the air as it passes over them, and the air will travel into all spaces where it will spread goodwill and compassion to all living things. So the flags are for the benefit of everyone and not just the person who hangs the flags. So, you should never hang flags to bring you blessings and luck, this would be driven by the ego; flags should be hung with altruism in mind. These flags are said to be 'Blessings spoken on the breath of nature'. Whether you believe in this sort of thing or not, it would be hard to deny the ethos of goodwill to all people. I would like to believe the flags work and so I hang flags when I can. But, if you've ever seen the movie 'Jaws' and heard the famous line: 'We're gonna need a bigger boat', well I think, 'We're gonna need a lot more flags', don't you?

Having explored the ridge, we worked our way back down to the lake to see if our boat was still there. It was and we paddled our way back to the other side. It was time for a beer. I loved sitting in the bars on the lakeside. They generally had low sofas, usually battered and it is fair to say a bit scruffy, but they were comfy and in the shade. I could have spent hours there drinking in the view and drinking in the beer, while admiring Phewa Lake, all the way up to the shining beacon that is the Peace Pagoda.

But Deb has always, had restless feet, and there comes a moment when we are away on holiday, or in this case on an adventure, when the inevitable gift shopping has to be done, and it drives me up the wall. Going from shop to shop Deb would speak those familiar words: "I wonder if what's her face would like this?" Then I would reply, "I don't know! Why don't we get everyone the same? It would make it quicker and easier?"

"You're no help at all, I'll do it."

We spent ages going to shops that all sold the same stuff. It wasn't all gift shopping though. I bought a few T-shirts. I wanted one with a map of the Annapurna Circuit embroidered on the back. I was going to get it before the start of the trek but thought it might tempt fate.

Deb liked the look of some silk scarves, and the guy invited us into his shop. He was an accomplished salesman. I usually can't stand salesmen trying to push a sale on you, but this guy was great. He was an older man with impeccable manners; a real gentleman, proper old school. He invited us to sit down, and he brought out the different scarves and placed them on wooden trestles so the light would catch them and we could see their true colours and the fine and intricate workmanship. They were gorgeous. It took a while for Deb to decide which ones she wanted, and then came the haggling. The price seemed okay to me, but Deb carried on until she was happy. He wrapped up our purchases and wished us luck. He was a nice guy and I'm glad we bought from his shop.

Deb was on a roll now and went looking for some walking trousers. She spied a pair she liked. Oh bugger, they were red! She haggled with the woman but to no avail. We came out of the shop without the trousers. Now that was a close call. "Let's go get a beer and a cocktail," I distracted her.

Back at the hotel, we got changed into clothes that weren't walking gear. It was such a good idea to bring clean clothes with us for when the trek was over. Out we went to cruise the main street and find somewhere to have a meal. We had eaten our fill of dhal bhat and veggie curries, even momos had lost their appeal. I suppose familiarity breeds contempt, and we just got bored of the same old food and fancied something different. It was dark now on the main street, and we looked through the windows of the different restaurants and food on offer. One caught our eye: Godfather's. It was an Italian restaurant with a real wood-fired oven. The flames could be seen at the back of the restaurant and the smell of freshly baked pizza was irresistible. In we went and ordered pizza, chips and beer; the food of champions. It was authentic Italian pizza and we ate until we were fit to burst, which wasn't a bad thing. We had both lost quite a lot of weight trekking the Circuit. I started the trek at 12 stone, and now I was about 10.5 stone. Deb had lost about a stone and was looking too skinny. So we both needed feeding up. We said when we do our next trek in Nepal, we will eat a lot more. Trekking would make a good weight-loss diet and exercise plan. Eat as much as you like, and walk 5 to 8 hours a day carrying a heavy pack, and you too could have a body like mine. Perhaps not! But you could lose a chunk of weight, get fit, and have a wonderful experience full of memories to relive around the fire on a cold winter's night, with a glass of good single malt whisky.

We discovered a great bar on the main street. It served Jamaican-style rum cocktails which were delicious. The bar was on the first floor and we managed to get seats outside on the veranda. This gave us a bird's eye view of the busy street below. It was happy hour, so two drinks for the price of one. We were by far the oldest people in the place, but Bob Marley was pumping out of the speakers, and this was music from our era, so we felt relaxed and at home. I paid a visit to the toilet which was at the back of the bar, and I walked past another room. I stopped to peer into the dimly lit smokey interior. There were several beds in there. There were no duvets or anything, just mattresses with young hippies lounging around on them. The pungent smell of cannabis wafted out into my face and that explained the relaxed and laid-back nature of the occupants of the room.

When I was younger I met someone who put me off the idea of taking drugs, and after that, I didn't feel comfortable taking anything risky. I was about 18 at the time and going through a hippy phase. The guy's name was Paul, and he was a couple of years older than me and was also a hippy. He told me his sad story. He used to take LSD, which is said to distort and alter a person's perception of reality; it is one of the most potent mood-altering drugs there is and commonly produces hallucinations. It is something a user has no control over. He had been using this drug for a few years and felt comfortable with it. He sometimes had a 'bad trip' but mostly he enjoyed it. However, his last trip was his worst trip. He thought he could fly, and he went to the top of a three-story building and launched himself off. I suppose that's when he discovered that he couldn't actually fly, and a little later he found that he couldn't walk either. That was the last time he took that drug, and since that day he has been in a wheelchair. It would be very easy to judge Paul and say it served the stupid bugger right. But there for the Grace of God go I. I'm not an expert in this field, and I might sound a bit naive, but I could have very easily gotten involved in drugs, and I thank God I didn't. I'm glad I met Paul and I hope he is doing okay now and enjoying life.

18

THE COFFEE MAN AND TROUBLE WITH MONKEYS

Whilst we were at the Peace Pagoda, we could see over to another hill; it was called Sarangkot. It is the place to go if you are into paragliding, and we saw a flock of them swooping around the top of the hill like giant vultures. Then some would peel away and land somewhere by the lake. So we thought we would get out of Pokhara for a while and climb up the hill and see the paragliders at close quarters. Rather than get a taxi to the bottom of the hill we decided to walk along the side of the road. This wasn't such a good idea as Nepalese roads aren't the easiest to walk beside and we were glad to get to the point where we could start the walk up the hill. We saw a wonderful sign at the bottom of the hill: 'No Smoking Zone, Instead Breathe Deeper In and Out - Sadhana Yoga'. Never mind nicotine gum and patches, this is the way to go. When you get the urge to have a fag, just breathe in and out until the urge passes. Sorted!

We zig-zagged our way up through rhododendron woods and farmland when we saw a guy sitting on a rock. As we approached him he greeted us with the usual,

"Namaste" and asked us how we were. He seemed a nice kind of guy so we stopped to chat with him. He said his name was Om and he owned a farm nearby where he grew coffee beans. I had drunk some Himalayan coffee in Pokhara and it tasted pretty good. He invited us to his farm for a coffee and we followed him through the fields. There was a German couple also walking up the hill, and he invited them too. We got to his farm and sat outside on a low wall while he busied himself making coffee and tea for Deb. While drinking our coffee it started to become clear why he had invited us here. He had guests stay here each year from all over the globe. They would make a donation to his farm and come and work in the fields for a week or sometimes even for a month. He would provide them with a room and food. The money would also help to send his children to school. He was very keen, and proud, to show us photographs of his daughter in her school uniform.

This guy was a natural salesman; he was very likeable and tried to convince us of his vision without being too pushy. But, the idea of buying expensive flights out to Nepal, making a large donation to his dream, and doing back-breaking work in the hot fields, all for just a hard mattress and a plate of dhal bhat, just wasn't doing it for us. And, his coffee was weak and tasted like piss. We contributed to the coffee and told him, "Good luck with your plans, but it's not our thing."

If the coffee had been good, it would have been a pleasant distraction from the hike up this hill in the heat. Still, it gave us a laugh. I find it hard to believe people would do this kind of thing, but Deb assures me they do. Maybe it's a form of masochism. Maybe these people derive sexual pleasure from working their bollocks off in the heat for next to nothing, while a little guy called Om orders them around.

I wonder if they work in their gimp costumes? There's a saying in Yorkshire: 'There's nowt queerer than folk', and that's probably true, but I suppose it's horses for courses too. Now I can see that might sound a bit uncharitable, but the coffee guy lived in a lovely spot and his children were going to school, and his whole situation seemed comfortable when compared to some of the poor buggers we have encountered on our travels. I'll save my charity for those who need it most, not this coffee farmer. Maybe he should use some of his money to learn the art of making a good cup of coffee.

We carried on up the hill and finally reached the top. I think Deb was tempted to have a try at the paragliding. Our daughter Grace has done a tandem paraglide, and she has also done a bungee jump. I would need to wear brown corduroy trousers if I had a go at either of these risky, adrenaline-filled activities. I don't believe the regulations and licensing for paragliding are the same in Nepal as in England. I think anybody can set up a business taking people for a flight. So I talked Deb out of it. If I went home with their Mum all mangled up from tumbling out of the sky, the kids would never forgive me. Still, it was great to watch them taking off. The view from the top was fantastic. Pokhara was spread out below with a population of about 500,000 people.

Making our way back down, we spied the 'coffee man' waiting for more tourists to lure back to his farm for a cup of piss. I wonder how many people he gets back to his farm each day? I suppose it's a bit like the scam emails I get; scammers must send out thousands of emails every day, and they only need to snare one or two unsuspecting people to make it a profitable enterprise. Bastards!

We took a different route back to Phewa Lake, which

avoided the busy road. This was much better and we soon reached the lake. While we were wandering along the walkway beside the lake, we saw a guy with a microphone and another with what looked like a TV camera. It appeared they were interviewing people. As we got closer it was obvious that they were going to stop us. My first thought was to say, 'No thanks, we're in a rush', which is my usual response to being confronted by salespeople on the street. But today I felt different about it. I would embrace my sociable side and join in whatever they were doing. It turned out that they worked for a local TV station and wanted to ask tourists about their experience of Nepal, and in particular Pokhara. But there was a twist to their interview. They would sing a traditional Nepalese song to us and we would have to say what we thought. At the end of the interview, we would have to sing a song to them. They sang their song and it was great, I like traditional stuff. Then they asked us about our trek and what we thought of Nepal. The questions were easy to answer because we had nothing negative to say, as we had both fallen in love with Nepal. However, all the time we were answering their questions, I was thinking about what song I would sing. The interview came to an end and they asked us to sing them a song. Deb is not much of a singer so she let me choose. I chose to sing the Bob Marley song 'No Woman No Cry'. This song seemed very appropriate as we have seen so many references to Bob Marley on our travels in Nepal. I'm not exactly sure why they have an obsession with Bob, but I would guess it is because his songs speak for the oppressed and the need for common people to stand together against those who would keep pushing them down into poverty. The Nepalese people are some of the poorest people in the world today. They live with a corrupt government that keeps them down. Bob speaks of freedom and rising up against corruption; he speaks for the downtrodden. So I can see why he has become such a hero to lots of people here. Perhaps I could have chosen a better song, but it was one I knew most of the words to. The exhibitionist in me came out and I belted it out. We soon drew a crowd and when I had finished, I revelled in the applause. I think I even took a bow.

It had been quite a strenuous morning and we were both feeling pretty hungry. It was a glorious day so we thought we would have a picnic on the lake. So we went shopping for some picnic food and a couple of cartons of juice. We went to the same place to hire our boat. It was less busy than before as the festival seemed to have finished. Taking turns rowing the boat we made our way to the opposite side of the lake where it was quieter. The sun was lovely and warm and we just let the boat drift while we had our packed lunch. I just love eating al fresco; it makes the food taste so much better and it becomes more of an event or occasion rather than just refuelling.

Moments like this are very special. We go hiking a lot in Mallorca in the mountains, and I remember one particular time, we had hiked up to a ridge from Soller called the Alfabia Ridge. Its height was 1067 metres and we walked up from nearly sea level so it was quite a hike. It took us about two hours to get to the top of the ridge. We ate our packed lunch there and sat on the warm rocks looking out to the turquoise sea. There was no breeze at all and the sun was warm. We stayed there for about an hour just watching the Egyptian vultures soaring past. It was the most beautiful view in all directions, mountain after mountain and all surrounded by the shining sea. We both agreed it was the best picnic spot in the world. Floating on the lake that afternoon was also a great picnic spot, and as we drifted about I put my head down for a couple of minutes to rest my eyes. I woke up an hour later with Deb rowing us back to shore.

Back at the hotel, it was time to do some packing. Tomorrow we will fly to Kathmandu. I can't say I was looking forward to it. Pokhara is such a laid-back place whereas Kathmandu is chaos central. The flight was a worry as well; it's not the actual bit in the air I mind, it's negotiating the airport to get on to the plane, and then getting from Kathmandu airport to a hotel, that bothered me. At least we would get to Kathmandu in the daylight this time if the flight is on time, which is never guaranteed in Nepal. After packing we went into town and had a meal, finishing at the Jamaican bar for happy hour and rum cocktails.

The next morning the alarm on my phone burst into life but it needn't have, as I was already awake. I had not slept very well thinking about the day of travelling we had in front of us. Breakfast for me was very minimal this morning but Deb had no such problem and had a hearty breakfast to set her up for the day's travel to come. We brought our luggage down to the lobby and the guy on reception rang for us a taxi. He had already negotiated a price for the taxi and told us it would be 500 rupees. We were sad to leave Pokhara and both vowed we would return one day. The taxi took us through the centre of town which was very different to the tourist area of Lakeside. In some ways, it was like any other large city. The differences were this city had cows walking in the road and instead of large branded shops like Marks and Spencer, it had small independent shops selling just about anything you could want.

Pokhara Airport is quite small as it only handles domestic flights. International flights are handled at Kathmandu. We were flying with Simrik Airlines but there was no one at their check-in desk yet, so we waited. I hate waiting. Should we sit down or should we stand in front of the desk? Since no one else was waiting we sat down. Then I noticed people around us also had the green Simrik tickets. I told Deb we should stand by the desk as there appeared to be quite a few people flying with our airline, and we needed to be at the front of the queue to make sure we got on the plane. Now I know this sounds a bit paranoid, but just because you are booked onto a flight does not mean you will get on it. There is a culture of 'first come first served' here, and it's no good arguing about it because this is just the way Nepal works. So we stood in front of the desk. Soon others got the idea and joined the queue.

The desk opened and we checked in. I always worry when they take our luggage away that it will be the last time we see it, but what choice did we have? From here we were directed to security. Deb had to go through the curtain with a female soldier and I went through the curtain with the male soldier. Well, they had green military uniforms on so they could have been soldiers or maybe police. They looked stern and official and carried large guns and enough weaponry to start a small war, which intimidated me. And, I hate it when we have to get split up. What if there is a problem with one of us and the other gets through okay? The stuff I worried about was infinite and my nerves were jangling.

We both got through security, okay, and we found where we thought the gate was for our flight. There seemed to be only two gates so that wasn't such an issue. We had read that boarding a plane could be a nightmare here so we were both surprised when it seemed to be going so easily. We could see the small planes landing, and then an official would call out the flight number. The people on the flight would queue up and be led out on the short walk to the plane. I say queue, but it doesn't seem to work like that here. People just gather around, a bit like going to a bar for a drink. There doesn't seem to be any organisation to it. People are quite prepared to push in and it doesn't bother their conscience one little bit.

Deb said she would like to sit on the left side of the plane as we would get a view of Mount Everest from that side. So I stealthily went into action; I slowly, but surely shuffled my way to just in front of the gate. We were now in pole position when our flight was called. And we didn't have long to wait. The official led us to the plane and, you guessed it, I was in front and the first to board the small, green plane. Result! The plane only seated 18 passengers. It had a line of single seats down one side and another down the other side with a narrow isle in the middle. I sat down on the left side and Deb sat in front. She was happy, therefore, so was I.

These planes don't hang about, and we were soon in the air. The flight attendant came around with a very small bottle of water and a boiled sweet. That was wonderful, but a bacon sandwich would have been better. The nerves were subsiding now and I was hungry, and I regretted not having a proper breakfast.

The views of the mountains were fantastic. Deb thought she had spotted Everest among the many mountains on view, but couldn't be sure. She took a million photos anyway, all with mountains and part of the aircraft wing intruding. The flight only lasted 30 minutes, and we touched down in Kathmandu.

We got off the little plane and made our way to the bag collection area. Where's the carousel? Where the fuck is the carousel? There wasn't a carousel. It was an old guy behind a counter with a massive crowd all trying to point out their bags. It was also my worst nightmare. Fuckity, fuckity, fuck! I realised, if I was polite and didn't push in, I would stay at the back of the crowd until Christmas. So I pushed and edged my way forward. I had already told Deb to wait away from the melee while I got the bags. At last, I was at the front. Now to catch the old guy's eye. This turned out to be easier than I had thought, probably because I was a good 12-inch taller than most of the people there and I think I was the only Westerner as well. I pointed to my bag and he lifted it onto the counter. I pointed out Deb's case and he did the same. It's a good job my adrenaline had kicked in because these two cases weighed 64 kilograms and I had to lift and push them through the crowd. I got the cases over to Deb and breathed a sigh of relief. Why the hell don't they have a proper carousel? That was just madness.

We have been through that airport since then, and they do now have a carousel. Perhaps the old guy retired, or more likely, died of exhaustion. Well, here we were back in the chaos that is Kathmandu. We walked past the taxi drivers plying their trade and went straight to the taxi office instead. We booked a taxi to take us to the Friends Home Hotel in the tourist district of Thamel. Kathmandu looked very different in the daylight; it was far less intimidating. The hotel was fully booked, but he rang the hotel round the corner and they had space. So we stayed at the hotel Osho Home Hotel.

Once settled in, we thought we would go out and explore Thamel. The air quality was horrendous; it was a mixture of diesel fumes and dust. Many of the locals wore face masks to prevent some of the nasty particulates from getting into their lungs, and it wasn't long before our eyes began to sting from the pollution and we both developed a cough. There is no happy medium in Nepal; in the mountains, the air is so clean and pure, but in Kathmandu, the air is like a soup of cancer-causing chemicals; it makes your eyes water and causes you to constantly cough like you have been smoking sixty fags a day for the last fifty years.

After the pollution, the next thing you notice is, the inability to stop; there is nowhere to sit down, and if you stop walking even for a second, you will be accosted by street vendors from every direction. They are everywhere and selling everything from Tiger Balm to traditional Nepalese instruments. After an hour of this, I was ready to burst and tell the vendors to 'Go fuck themselves'. I didn't do this, Deb would have killed me. After all, they have to make a living, and this is their city and their place of work, we're just passing through. It's worth looking down some of the narrower streets as sometimes you can find, as we did, a quieter coffee shop. It is wonderful to be able to sit down away from the noise of the traffic and relax.

Before we came to Kathmandu, I used to believe it would be a much smaller place; more like a small, medieval town where the only traffic was horses and it would be full of ancient cultural relics. That vision couldn't be further from the truth. Modern Nepal is not like that at all. Although it has lots of ancient buildings, most of this vast city is industrialised, dirty and above all frantically busy with thousands of people trying to eke out a living. I couldn't live in Kathmandu; it would drive me insane. A few days of visiting would be great but any longer would be unbearable. Give me the rural side of Nepal, up in the mountains, any day. Sitting there in that coffee shop, both of us agreed, that we wished we were back on the Annapurna Circuit, carrying our packs amongst the lovely mountains.

We went out for a meal in the evening. I Googled restaurants and found one pretty close to our hotel. It was called

Gaia and was only a five-minute walk away. The evening was warm and we sat in a courtyard lit by hundreds of candles. Our meal was delicious and the service was friendly and efficient. I know that sounds like a Trip Advisor review, but it was a five-star kind of place for two-star prices. We would revisit Gaia again before we left for home.

We had made a plan for our first full day in Kathmandu, so after an early breakfast we set off. First, we would visit the 'Monkey Temple' and then over to 'Durber Square'. It's about two miles to the 'Monkey Temple' so we decided to walk. It's not easy navigating your way through the rabbit warren of streets and alleys, and we got lost a few times. People are very helpful though and were happy to point us in the right direction. It feels like there must be a million motorbikes in Kathmandu, and every one of them has tried to push past us in the narrow alleyways. Beep bloody beep! Surely they can bring in a law that prohibits motorbikes from riding on the footpaths. I complained a lot about this, and I think Deb found me as annoying as the bikes. Our Tom would have accepted the bikes, 'It's their culture Dad', I can hear him say. Well, it might be their culture, but it's my sodding feet they're running over.

We followed a main road over a bridge that crossed a river. If you can call it a river; it was more like an open sewer. One of my passions is fly fishing, and I love spending time by the river. It doesn't matter whether I catch a trout or not, it's just great to be in lovely natural surroundings. Seeing this filthy, sewage-ridden river was upsetting. How can people allow such filth and devastation to happen? Then we noticed something even more upsetting. On the bank of the river were several huts. They were cobbled together with bits of wood and polythene and pieces of discarded rubbish. We couldn't believe that these were dwellings. People actually lived here! It was incredulous that human beings lived in such squalor. This was poverty in its most desperate, and unacceptable, form. Once again my protestations evaporated away, and I was moved to tears. Sometimes I am an ungrateful arse. I have everything, and some people have absolutely nothing at all. The clothes I was wearing probably cost more money than these people will see in their short lifetimes. I felt ashamed as we walked on over the bridge.

The 'Monkey Temple' is built on top of a hill with hundreds of steps to climb to get up there. As the name suggests, there are lots of monkeys about. The Nepali name of the temple is 'Swayambhunath Stupa', but tourists to the area named it 'Monkey Temple', probably because it's easier to pronounce and there are lots of monkeys about. Myth has it that the whole of the Kathmandu Valley was once a lake, and in that lake grew a lotus flower, which morphed into the Monkey Temple. The name 'Swayambhu' means self sprung. The temple is one of the most revered sites for Buddhist pilgrims and is also an important site for Hindus. It is believed to have been built in the 5th century, so it is a very ancient site. However, the monkeys wandering freely around were a distraction to me.

I have a bit of a phobia about monkeys, and I think I know why. I have an old photograph of when I was about 8 years old. It was taken in Scarborough by one of those photographers who would accost tourists by plonking a monkey, or a parrot, on some unsuspecting kid and take their photograph. Of course, the parents would want to buy the picture of their offspring being tormented by a semi-wild creature. What kind of person makes a living out of putting the fear of God into kids, and then asking them to smile while they photograph them? Evil bastards that's who!

Well, I think that's where my phobia began. Several years later, when I was 15, in my first job, the foreman dressed up in a gorilla suit he was going to a fancy dress party in. He jumped up onto the work benches doing his best gorilla impression. I was freaked out; my head was telling me 'It's not a real gorilla, it's just Terry the foreman', but my heart was saying, 'GORILLA - RUN LIKE FUCK!'. As I said, monkeys scare me. And there were lots of monkeys here: little ones, females ones with babies attached, and big buggers with red arses. Every one of them gave me the heebie-jeebies. It said in the 'Welcome to Nepal' blurb: 'Find Peace and Prayers at Swayambhunath'. There was no peace here for me, not with these devilish monkeys roaming about looking to mug someone.

We wandered around the Stupa and saw some people worshipping before alters. This usually involves all five senses: hearing - a bell is rung to awaken the deity; taste - a gift of food is offered; sight - the image of the deity is shown; smell - incense is burned or flowers present; touch - powder is placed on the forehead to remind the devotee of their devotion throughout the day. This worship is very touchy-feely and looks like fun. Unlike Christian services where you sit for an hour singing hymns, that are a hundred years old, while getting a numb arse from the hard wooden pews. The whole Church of England service has become too sanitised, while the Hindu worship is vibrant, colourful and in your face, full of smells and fire. Church of England services are very sterile compared to the ones we are witnessing. Even the communion wine is non-alcoholic. I'm pretty sure when Jesus taught his disciples the meaning of bread and wine, in the act of remembrance, he used full-fat wine and not pretend wine at zero per cent.

I was relieved to go back down from the hill. We called

in a very westernised coffee shop for a drink and a bite to eat. It was hard work this sightseeing. The temperature was rising now but we still decided to walk back and go to the World Heritage Site of Durbar Square. There is an admission fee to enter the Square, and as soon as you are in you get bombarded by people wanting to guide you around. The conversation usually goes like this: "Namaste. Where are you from?" The hopeful guide would say.

"We're from England." We would reply

"Ah! I have family who live in England." The guide would continue.

"Oh, which part of England do they live in?"

"I'm not sure. Which part do you live in?"

"Yorkshire."

"Ah, I remember now. They live in Yorkshire too."

"Amazing! But we don't want a guide."

Occasionally we would pretend to come from some obscure place like Belize, but the same kind of conversation took place, we would just make up a fictitious area in Belize.

Durbar Square is quite overwhelming. The buildings are intricate and very old. The earthquake in 2015 caused so much damage to them, and many have supporting, wooden struts to stop them from falling down. If this were back home in the UK, it would be fenced off from the public by the Health and Safety brigade. I don't usually agree with most of what these people deem to be dangerous, but in the case of the buildings in Durbar Square, I think they would have a point. They look like a strong gust of wind would blow them down. There were many people here worshipping at the various shrines, so it was very much a working site. You're either there as a tourist or there to take part in worship. There are many 'holy men' here, known as Sadhus. Interesting title. They are dressed in yellow, gold and orange. Usually, they have their faces also painted in these colours. All have very long beards. It is said that Sadhus are trying to break the cycle of death and rebirth. One asked us if we would like to touch his beard. We declined his kind offer; it's not our thing touching beards. We did see others touching it though. As soon as they did, the holy man would hold out his hand for a donation. It's not cheap touching holy beards for a blessing. I'm glad we gave it a miss, I'm blessed enough.

We saw a crowd of very excited people carrying what looked like a throne on their shoulders with a young girl sitting on it. We had read about this. She was regarded as a living goddess. She is a Kumari, which means 'prepubescent girl' and she has been selected from the Shakya caste of the Nepalese Newari Buddhist community. It is believed that Devi Mahatmyam, the goddess, declared she would live inside all females. However, only young virgins are chosen because of their purity. It is said that the Kumari can heal the sick. Once she has been chosen, she walks across Durbar Square to her palace where she will live until she is no longer able to be a Kumari. That will be when she starts her first period. Until then, if she leaves her palace she must be carried everywhere.

We saw her being carried along and followed the crowd. They went into an old building which had a very ornate courtyard. Deb tried to take a photograph but was jumped on angrily by devotees close by, "NO PHOTOS!", they shouted furiously. We took the hint and left. It must be a strange life being a Kumari. I wonder how they feel when their time as a goddess ends. How difficult would it be to adapt to being just ordinary again? It has got to mess with their minds and give them mental health issues. I can just hear them say, "What! You want me to sweep up? Fuck off! I used to be a living goddess you know". Yes, life must be strange after you've been a goddess incarnate.

Exploring further, we took our lives in our hands and went inside some of the buildings. Many are palaces and are guarded by armed soldiers. But, it all got a bit much after a while; there's only so much history and religious stuff you can look at before you start to yearn for a cold beer. As we walked back through the square to head back to Thamel, somebody was feeding the pigeons. There were hundreds of them, and a vendor would sell you corn to feed them. It made a very photogenic scene, and we took a few photos. Deb's Grandad 'Tommy' used to call pigeons 'Flying rats', and looking at the thousands flying and shitting everywhere, I think he might have had a point. This place was full of very well-fed flying rats all doing their best to shit on my head. I was quite glad to leave the holy square.

We called in at Gaia and sat in the shade drinking a cold Everest beer and reflecting on our first day in Kathmandu. It is a place that cannot be ignored; it is full-on and in your face. We went back to the hotel to get cleaned up, then went out for a pizza. And, a couple more beers of course. We had heard that there is a pizza restaurant called Fire and Ice that is worth a visit, so we gave it a try. It was a good pizza, and it gave us a chance to sit down and discuss what we would do tomorrow.

19

I SEE DEAD PEOPLE

More cultural stuff today. Yes, we're a right pair of culture vultures now. We're going to Boudhanath, which is a giant stupa, and then to Pashupatinath, where by the river, the dead are cremated. Boudhanath is a fair walk from Thamel, so we opted for a taxi. Most of the taxis seem to be old Suzuki Swifts, and they have seen better days; I suspect most of them have been around the clock a few times. There are lots of garages doing repairs around the city keeping the mechanics busy and the old taxis on the road. The rules of the road in Kathmandu are only applied very loosely. The traffic is manic and driving is not for the faint-hearted. The noise of car horns is incessant, but it's not due to road rage. It's just letting others know they are coming through. I can honestly say we didn't see one incident of road rage on the entire trip. This is in sharp contrast to the UK, where road rage is an everyday occurrence.

We were dropped off at the main entrance to the Boudhanath complex and paid our entrance fee. We later realised, we could have gone down one of the streets adjacent to the entrance and walked in for free. Nepal can be crazy that way sometimes. There were many beggars around the Stupa. Some of them looked in a terrible state. One particular man was dressed in rags; there were more holes in his clothing than there was fabric, and he was filthy. But, the most striking aspect of his appearance was he had no legs, and he dragged himself around on a piece of plastic. We have seen beggars in Paris, Rome and our home city of Leeds, but none of them were in the same league as these beggars. They were as desperate as any human being could be, and we tried to give each of them a few rupees.

The Boudhanath Stupa is enormous; the sheer size of it is mesmerising. There has been a stupa here for about 1500 years. Its origin is shrouded in the mists of time. However, where hard facts are missing myths abound. And, mythology has it that King Vikramaditya built a well at his palace, but it produced no water. He consulted astrologers for advice and they said that to bring water to the well, a male human sacrifice must be made. However, it couldn't be just any male. The male sacrifice must have 32 perfections, and the only candidates with 32 perfections for the sacrifice, were the King and his two Princes. The King decided to make himself the sacrifice and ordered one of his sons to do the deed. However, he didn't tell the Prince that it would be himself that was being sacrificed. Instead, he said the man to be sacrificed would be sleeping, with his body and head covered by a cloth, and should not be woken. The Prince cut the sleeping man's head off only to find it was his father the King. Horrified, he asked the priests what he could do to redeem himself from this hideous act. They told him to cast a chicken from a certain building, and wherever it landed he should build a stupa. He did this and the chicken landed where the Boudhanath now stands.

You couldn't make this stuff up. Where on earth would you find a male with 32 perfections? And, so what, your well doesn't produce water, it doesn't mean you have to lose your head to get some. It's just not worth dying for, just use a different well instead. I do love mythological tales though; you never know which way they're going to go. I'm sure the people who made them up were taking an early form of LSD or maybe eating magic mushrooms.

Some steps lead up to the plinth of the stupa. From here you can see devotees prostrating themselves in acts of worship, and others circumambulating around the outside of the stupa in an anticlockwise direction. This direction is traditional, and if you walk the other way round you can certainly tell you are going against the current. I like to go against the current; following the crowd has never been my attitude to life, and I believe you should plough your own furrow. But if you did that here you would bump into lots of people, and it would take a long time to get around as well.

Prayer flags, ornate bells of every size chained together, lighted candles and people performing puja. The whole site was alive with religion, but it sat comfortably alongside the secular activities of those just going about their daily business. While walking around the stupa high on the plinth, I spotted a 'Himalayan Coffee Company' coffee shop. It was on the second floor and enormous inside. We couldn't get a window seat but that was okay as there was lots of people-watching to be done inside. There were groups of monks, dressed in their red robes, who sat at tables having breakfast. This sparked a debate between Deb and myself.

Some of the monks were eating bacon, and I thought that Buddhists were vegetarian. Deb didn't think they had to be. But I remember seeing the film '7 Years in Tibet' with Brad Pitt. He was constructing a building for the Dhali

Lhama, and when they dug out the foundations they had to do it very carefully and remove all the worms alive from the excavated soil. It was a, 'No worms were harmed, in the making of this building', kind of thing. So I believed that Buddhists didn't kill or harm living creatures, and hence were also vegetarians. I later did some research and found that Chinese and Vietnamese Buddhists are strict vegetarians, but others are not condemned for eating meat. There you go, Deb was right again. Bugger! One day it will be my turn to be right.

We spent about 2 hours at the Boudhanath and then decided to walk to Pashupatinath. We looked at our map, took a general direction with a compass and set off through the hot dusty streets. And they were hot. After what seemed like a very long time, and still, Pashupatinath was not in sight, we flagged down a taxi. He dropped us at a bridge and we followed the river path. The Bagmati River is meant to be holy and it is on its banks that bodies are cremated and then the ashes are carried away by the river. I'll be honest, the river didn't look too holy to me, there was too much plastic waste and litter floating on it for that, and it was a cloudy green colour. The ashes are carried by this river which eventually meets the Holy Ganges River. We saw the stone plinths where the cremations would take place, but there were no funerals today. I normally hate funerals, but morbidly I was hoping to see one here today. Usually at funerals, you see the coffin disappear behind a curtain, accompanied by weird, spooky, music, and that's it. You all go to the pub and eat pork pies and cheese sandwiches while someone incinerates the fuck out of your loved one. It might be just me, but don't you feel there is a disconnect there? At least with open cremations, like these at the holy river, you actually see your loved one literally go up in smoke. Maybe death has become too sanitised in the West. The native Americans place their dead on high platforms for the birds to devour. This is a very green way of recycling your loved one. Maybe when I die they can stick me on the roof and let the magpies pick at me. But, I don't think the council would allow it somehow. Councils are like that where we live.

I don't think you ever forget the first time you see a dead person. I was 18 when I saw mine. It was my first day as a gravedigger. I had been out on a heavy drinking session with my mates the night before and I had a massive hangover; I threw up several times before setting off for the cemetery. The head guy wanted to show me around before I got started. The first building we went into was where the grass cutters were and other tools, including the spade which I would need pretty soon. The second building was an entirely different kettle of fish; it was where autopsies took place and bodies were held in cold storage. The smell of strong disinfectant greeted us as we walked in, which made me feel sick, and I had to concentrate hard to keep it together and not disgrace myself. The stainless steel dissection table had been recently washed down, but I could still see traces of watery blood on it. It was a grim place. Then I was shown the cold storage. My new boss opened one of the long drawers and pulled out an old man. He was covered by a white sheet which he pulled back to reveal the corpse's face. His skin was a grey, white, almost translucent colour. My first thought was 'What the hell is he doing in here? He'll freeze'.

I've seen other dead people since then, but you never forget your first. Later that afternoon I had to dig my first grave. The boss showed where it was to be dug. If it had not been in the middle of the cemetery, it could have been excavated with a small JCB digger. Unfortunately for me, the grave was surrounded by headstones, so it had to be dug by hand with a spade. He marked the area out where I should dig. I said, "How deep do I dig down?"

"You'll know when to stop when you hit the coffin that's already down there," he replied with a smirk on his face.

I said, "What coffin?" with a look of dread on my face.

He explained that there had been a family member buried there 14 years ago. "What if the coffin is rotted? Will I dig down into the body?" I asked him.

"Hopefully not, usually there are stone flags which have been put on top of the coffin, but you won't know that until you get down there," he replied.

At that point, I should have told him to stick the job up his arse and gone home. I didn't, and the next few hours were some of the toughest hours I have ever worked. It was August and the sun was blazing down. I started digging. At first, it was okay, it was when the grave got deeper that it got really hard. I had to dig the soil into a bucket and lift it out of the hole by climbing a small ladder. I got down to about 6 feet. I knew it was 6 feet because I was about 6 feet tall and the grave closed in around me. The sun beat down on me in this fucking grave and I was shitting myself that I would fall through into the rotten coffin below and the decaying corpse inside. Crack! I hit concrete flags. Thank God for that! That wasn't the last time I would stand over an old long-buried coffin.

I didn't stay in the grave digging job long. Instead, I got a job landscaping an old graveyard. I think I must have an affinity with graveyards. At the time I didn't have a problem with this, but I now realise that it should have been left as it was; a wild, overgrown place that was a wildlife sanctuary. By the time we had finished the job, it was a grassed area with no character and completely void of any wildlife. Some might say it looked manicured and well-kept. I would say where are the birds going to nest, and where are the insects going to live? We had created a sterile environment not fit for man or beast. The seventies weren't a good time for conservation where we lived.

Anyway, I started work on the landscaping process. We were taking down the old tombstones and gravestones, and using them to make walkways. The tombs had to be filled in to prevent heavy machinery, such as grass-cutting vehicles, from breaking through in the future. Most of this was pretty straightforward. The last occupants were buried here over a hundred years ago or more. It was just a matter of lifting the top slab off and then using a heavy three-metre metal pole to smash through into the other levels. This caused it all to collapse and then it could be filled in with hard core. However, we came across a recent internment where the last occupant had only been down there for nine years. We lifted the top slab and immediately the stench hit us. It was the smell of putrified flesh and made everyone within 5 metres gag. The vicar was called for, and he blessed the corpse and permitted us to carry on filling in the tomb. Maybe he should have blessed us at the same time, or at least splashed us with holy water. Preferably scented holy water. Rose water would have been nice.

I was given the job of straddling the grave. I placed one foot on each side and stood holding the heavy pole ready to break through the slabs underneath. I had a scarf around my nose and mouth, but I still held my breath. The first attempt to smash through didn't succeed, so I took a minute before I tried again. I can still remember looking down into that grave and imagining the corpse looking up at me. I drove the pole down again and again, all the while trying to hold my breath, when at last, the slab gave way, and the coffin and stone slabs collapsed down into the void. The guy in the dumper truck was ready to empty the hardcore, and it was done. I think that has to rank among one of the trickiest moments in my working life. It's up there with teaching electricity to the bottom set year 11 on a Friday afternoon.

Seeing these aspects of death made me want to be cremated when I eventually shuffle off this mortal coil. So if any of my family are reading this, DO NOT PUT ME INTO A HOLE. Burn me to a crisp and scatter my ashes on the moors of the Yorkshire Dales, where the air is sweet and clear, the breeze can blow right through me, and I can see for miles and miles. That'll do! That'll do!

Pashupatinath is not just a place for funerals, it is also a place of worship. We paid for admission and climbed up the steps to explore the complex of ancient temples. As with all the temples we have visited in Nepal, they are not just historical relics, they are used for daily worship. But, Pashupatinath is a very special place. It is revered by Hindus as a place to die. Many elderly Hindus come here to spend their last few weeks in the temple's shelters before they die. It is believed that dying here will allow them to be reborn as a human, regardless of any sins or bad karma they may have acquired. So Hindus from all over Nepal and India come here to die and be cremated.

Another surprising sight to see is local women washing clothes downstream of the cremation site. It is said the water here contains animal fat as a result of the cremated bodies, and that this fat helps to wash dirty linen. Some say this is how soap was invented. We didn't see any of the washerwomen, but if we had, I wouldn't have given them my underpants to wash, I'll stick to Daz thank you very much.

Many of the temples are dedicated to the Hindu god

Shiva, and the main temple has a huge golden statue of Nandi, which is Shiva's bull, but only Hindus are allowed into the main temple, so we never got to see it. But, lots of the smaller shrines and sacred places are also devoted to Shiva. These are easy to distinguish as they are adorned by lingams. These lingams are erect phalluses and they are the symbol of Shiva and they can be seen everywhere around the temple complex. I never realised that so many of the lads I have taught over the years were followers of Shiva, but there in the back of their exercise books, there would always be lingams of all shapes and sizes. Teenage lads are completely obsessed with lingams.

We caught a taxi to a place just outside the Thamel area. It was a lovely place called 'The Garden Of Dreams'. We had to pay a small admission fee to get in. This provided another example of Nepalese bureaucracy. We paid our fee and were given two tickets. Then there was a guy in uniform, only an arm's length from where we bought the tickets, who had to inspect and verify the tickets before stamping them so we could pass into the garden.

Inside it was like another world. The walls are very high and it seems to dampen down the noise from the busy streets outside. Outside is full of litter and dust, inside it is calm, peaceful and clean. The whole design is very European and is like walking into an Edwardian garden. There are pavilions, ponds and pergolas. Everything has an ornate opulence to it, like something from a bygone era. The lawns are green and very well-kept. It was very easy to imagine a game of cricket being played on them. There were lots of people here but it didn't feel busy or full. Courting couples found the more secluded benches to sit on, while many availed themselves of the yoga-style mats to lay on the grass. It was such a relaxing atmosphere that I put my arm around Deb and kissed her on the cheek. From her reaction, you wouldn't have been blamed for thinking it was Judas betraying Jesus with a kiss. "We can't do that here!" she said sharply. Public displays of affection are not socially acceptable in Nepal. Even when I held Deb's hand she got worried we would offend people.

I told her "We have been holding hands since we started courting, we're not going to stop now." Sometimes it was just safer to hold hands, like crossing the busy roads or walking the dark streets in the evening. I know it's their culture, but surely holding hands, and maybe a peck on the cheek, isn't going to offend anybody. The strange thing is you often see men with their arms around each other on the streets, but you can't do the same with a woman. You figure that one out.

There was even a photographer here with a model bride and groom, probably taking pictures to put on his website. Many were having picnics but we decided to give the restaurant a try. We only wanted a light snack. It was a very posh place, and the staff wore white formal dress and bow ties. It was like going to Betty's in Harrogate; very posh. I'm glad we only had a light snack though, because the prices were astronomical. But, it was our last day before we headed home, so why not? And, we needed to use our rupees as we wouldn't be able to exchange them back at home. It was the most expensive meal we have had while in Nepal. While we waited for our meal, we read in our guidebook about the Garden of Dreams. It was built in 1920 and was originally called the 'Garden of Six Seasons'. It was built for Field Marshal Kaiser Sumsher Rana (1892-1964). After he died in 1964 it fell into disrepair and was neglected for many years until recently, when it was restored to its former glory with the help of the Austrian government. We delved deeper to find out why the garden was originally called 'The Garden Of Six Seasons'. Nepalese believe they have six seasons instead of four. This may seem a little strange, but Nepal, being a very mountainous country, has 5 different climatic zones: below 1200 metres it is the tropical and subtropical zone; the temperate zone lies between 1200 to 2400 metres; the cold zone is between 2400 and 3600 metres; the sub-arctic zone is from 3600 to 4400 metres; and the artic zone is above 4400 metres. So there is a massive variation in altitude throughout Nepal and this affects the climate. The six seasons are:

Spring (mid-March to mid-May) is also known as the windy season

Early summer (mid-May to mid-July)

Summer monsoon (mid-July to mid-Sep)

Early autumn(mid-Sep to mid-Nov)

Late autumn(mid-Nov to mid-Jan) also called pre-winter

Winter (mid-Jan to mid-March)

I like the idea of six seasons, but I'm not too sure how it would work in Yorkshire, where we sometimes have four seasons in one day.

We walked back into Thamel and did some last-minute gift shopping. Tonight was our last night in Kathmandu, and tomorrow we would begin the long flight home. Because it was our last night we thought we would go to our favourite restaurant, Gaia. It was a good night and we reflected on our journey; from trekking the Annapurna Circuit to Pokhara and finally to getting to know Kathmandu. It had a feeling of being a full stop; drawing a line under the whole adventure. I know it would be a couple of days before we got home, but hopefully, that would be pretty straightforward. Or was I being too optimistic? Things are never quite that straightforward when we travel.

20

HOMEWARD BOUND

The following morning we paid our hotel bill and loaded our bags into the taxi. It had been good staying at the Osho Home Hotel and we thanked the hotel staff for looking after us and vowed if we came back to Kathmandu we would stay here again.

Tribhuvan International Airport in Kathmandu is a daunting place. We found the check-in desk and joined the queue. Then the queue morphed into a crowd, and we all funnelled into a narrow stream to the desk. It took ages, and we needed to constantly assert our position. I was reminded of the old navy saying, 'Hold Fast'. This is a normal way of life for the Nepalese, but it was alien to us. We tried to keep a smile on our faces and go with the flow. Finally, we got to the front and dropped our bags off, then made our way to security, of which there were several barriers to go through; men one way and women the other. At each barrier, an official stamped our boarding passes. It was like an orienteering exercise, but not as much fun.

At last, we made it through and were reunited. For an

international airport, it was very basic; no shops selling whisky and perfume, no fast food outlets, not even a Costa, just row upon row of seating most of them with people sitting on them. It was just a waiting game now. And we waited and waited and waited. The aircraft eventually arrived and we began to board. The whole system was so slow. And it didn't help once we were aboard. People were just wandering around taking selfies. The aircrew were trying to get people strapped in before we took off but no one seemed to care, except Deb and me. We had a quick turnaround at Abu Dhabi and we were already cutting it fine. I felt like shouting, 'For God's sake sit down or get off the fucking plane'.

When the plane eventually took off, we held hands. This is a routine we have had for years. I suppose it's just in case everything goes tits up and we fall out of the sky. At least we do so together. I think it's a habit brought on by an accident we had before we were married. We were having a heated row in the car while driving home. Take my advice and never row while you are driving, it's far too dangerous. I was turning right at a particularly difficult bend in the road. As I pulled out a large Ford Granada, going way too fast, smashed into the driver's side. We both saw the car coming and screamed "I love you." Luckily we survived with cuts and bruises. When push comes to shove, the only thing that matters at all is love. And, that's why we hold hands on take off. If the plane were to crash and burn, and we hurtled headlong into oblivion, we would go down hand in hand screaming "I love you."

Time dragged by. Would we make our other flight? What happens if we miss it? As usual, Deb tried to keep me calm and told me that whatever happens, it will all work itself out. Of course, she was right, but it didn't stop my stomach from being tied in knots. I was like a coiled spring, ready to explode.

We landed at Abu Dhabi airport, and we were late. I told Deb, "As soon as we get off the plane, we'll find out where we need to go then RUN."

And that's what we did. It took about 10 minutes to get to the next gate, and when we got there it had just closed. And, I do mean JUST closed. I asked the staff at the gate if they could just let us get on. We could see the plane just outside of the window. It was right there. "Why can't we just get on now?" I said with frustration-induced thunder in my voice. The answer they gave us was a very polite and calm, no. I'm afraid I did the stupid thing that you should never do. I said, "I am appalled and I will never fly with your airline again." Deb did her best to calm me down but I had gone into meltdown. When I look back now, I can see how wrong I was, but at the time I was seeing red. The coiled spring had been sprung. I know it's no excuse, and I hold my hand up to being a complete arse.

The next flight was in 10 hours, and we were given a room in a hotel to wait it out. We boarded a minibus, with others who had missed their flights and were taken to a swanky hotel on the outskirts of Abu Dhabi. The room was more than adequate and we were given a free buffet-style meal. I had a shower in our room and calmed down. I even watched a film on the TV. It was 'Paddington 2'. If it ever comes on TV now, I watch it as it reminds me of our stay in Abu Dhabi. Weird eh? This situation wasn't so bad. Okay, it was a wait of 10 hours, but we had our room and they fed us well. After that, we had a short sleep, before we were driven back to the airport and eventually made it onto the last flight home.

Manchester was dark, cold and rainy when we landed.

We headed for the railway station and bought our tickets for Leeds. As we were early, we were the only two on the platform. It was cold and we were tired. It wasn't as cold as Thorong La, but the dampness in the air, and the gloomy surroundings, somehow made it feel much colder. The train filled up with people commuting to work, and we tried, in vain at times, to stay awake. The commuters, in their smart work clothes, had no idea that we had been to the Himalayas and walked around the Annapurna Circuit. We probably just looked like a couple of holidaymakers coming home from a week in Alicante, still sodden with sangria.

We arrived in Leeds and caught a taxi to take us home. Our house was still standing, so that was a bonus. We stumbled through the door with our bags. "Put the kettle on Dave," said Deb. "We're home."

THE END

EPILOGUE

Do you know that feeling you get when you come home after a holiday? It takes a few days to shake off that holiday feeling and get back to normal life. "This time last week we were..." is something you catch yourself saying for days after you get back home. Well, coming home after an adventure is just the same sensation but on steroids. I think we both had post-adventure blues for weeks afterwards. I sorted out the millions of photos we had taken and ordered a photo book. I was also hooked on YouTube videos of the Annapurna Circuit. It gave me a real thrill to see the places we had been to. But, also a melancholia and a yearning to be back there. However, it was very interesting to see that nearly all of the videos covered only part of the full circuit. Most started way after Besisahar and finished at Jomson. If after reading this book we have inspired you to do the Circuit, and you have the time, please do the full Circuit, you won't regret it.

On our return, we visited our kids and told them all about the trek and thanked them again for paying for it. I was grateful that they 'pushed' me out of my comfort zone.

Kids learn a lot from their parents, but it works the other way around as well, I have learned a lot from them. Bless 'em all!

I miss meeting new people and being in the mountains. I miss admiring the fantastic views and spending quality time with Deb without the interruption of everyday life. But the thing that I miss most is the freedom that trekking brings. It's the simple existence of getting up each day and just walking; just putting one foot in front of the other, in the clear air with a clear mind. Deb and I both agreed that we have to go back to Nepal and do some more trekking. We don't know when, but we must go back. There are so many treks to do and so many mountains to see, and we aren't getting any younger, so we had better get a move on.

In 2019 we returned to Nepal and did an extended trip around the Everest region. We decided against flying into Lukla, and so we trekked the old route into the Everest area from a place called Jiri. It took a week to get to the Lukla area. Then we trekked to Gokyo, from where we crossed over a high pass called Cho La. Here we joined the main trail to Everest Base Camp and Kala Patthar. This was a new high for us as the peak of Kalapathar is at a height of 5645 metres. From here we trekked over to the Chukhung Valley and walked to Island Peak Base Camp. From there we went to Ama Dablam Base Camp. I suppose we thought, why do one base camp when you can do three? Then down, down, down back to Lukla, the most dangerous airport in the world, and a flight to Kathmandu. It took us 31 days of trekking. Again, we did it all self-guided and carried our own packs.

I didn't think any trek could surpass the Annapurna Trek, but this one did just that. It was amazing, and we can't wait to go back and strap on our packs, pull on our boots, and walk those mountains again.

I used to think Nepal was way out of my comfort zone. And it was. Now I feel at home there and can't wait to return to the beautiful Himalayas, just me and my Deb.

ACKNOWLEDGMENTS

I must thank the many trekkers we met on our adventure all of whom entertained and informed us in equal measure. The staff and owners of the many lodges we stayed in were wonderful and provided us with information, food and shelter always with smiles on their faces. Thanks as to go to Kieran and Helena for their company and friendship. However, my biggest thanks must go to Deb. She kept me going when things got tough. She was always there and she is my hero.

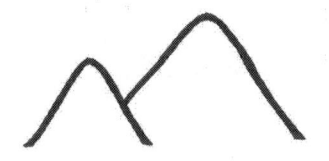

Printed in Great Britain
by Amazon